CONRAD AND IMPERIALISM

By the same author

DELUSIONS AND DISCOVERIES:
Studies on India in the British Imagination

CONRAD AND IMPERIALISM

Ideological Boundaries and Visionary Frontiers

Benita Parry

First published 1983 by
THE MACMILLAN PRESS LTD
London and Basingstoke
Companies and representatives
throughout the world

ISBN 0 333 27083 5

Typeset in Great Britain by
Wessex Typesetters Ltd
Frome, Somerset
Printed in Hong Kong

Contents

Blind, fooled and staggering from her throne, I saw her fall,
Clutching at the gaud of Empire;
And wondering round her, sons and daughter-nations stood –
What madness had possessed her;
But when they lifted her, her heart was dead,
Withered within the body, and all the veins
Were choked with yellow dirt.

Edward Carpenter, *'Empire' in Toward Democracy*, 1902

Here I lay it down that Imperialism . . . is to be taken as the typical symbol of the end. Imperialism is pure civilization. In this outward form the destiny of the West is now irrevocably set. The energy of culture-man is directed inwards, that of civilization-man outwards. For this reason I see in Cecil Rhodes the first man of the new epoch. He represents the political style of a Western, Teutonic, particularly German future. His phrase 'expansion is everything' contains in its Napoleonic form the most real tendency of every mature civilization . . . It is not a matter of choice. It is not the conscious will of individuals or of whole classes or peoples that decides. The expansive tendency is a fate, something daemonic and huge which grips, forces into service and consumes the late mankind of the world-city stage, whether it wills it or not, whether it knows it or not.

Oswald Spengler, *The Decline of the West*, 1918

Acknowledgements

I wish to thank the British Museum for providing a microfilm of 'The Rescuer' manuscript and allowing permission to quote, also Faber and Faber Ltd and Random House Inc. for permission to quote 'In Memory of W. B. Yeats' from *Collected Poems* by W. H. Auden.

Thanks also to the staff of Warwick University Library for their hospitality to a persistent visitor and in particular to Audrey Cooper for considerable help; to Julia Steward for her sympathetic editing, to Terri Moss for preparing the typescript, to Jeremy Gray and Sue Laurence for their comments, and to Bill and Rachel for their companionship.

B.P.

1 Introduction

Conrad in his 'colonial fictions' did not presume to speak for the colonial peoples nor did he address them, and if this aloofness is registered in portraits of iconic figures posed against archetypal landscapes, it also spared his writing the excess of that sentimentality joined with paternalistic reproof which was a characteristic feature of the nineteenth-century colonial novel. His original constituents were the subscribers to *Blackwood's* and *New Review*, an audience still secure in the conviction that they were members of an invincible imperial power and a superior race, and his contemporary readers remained those to whom colonial possessions appeared a natural extension of their own national boundaries. The extent to which Conrad in his own day, when he was hailed as the Kipling of the Seas, succeeded in his ambition to make his readers *see*, cannot be gauged; what is verifiable is that he was popularly regarded as a writer of romances in faraway places and stirring tales of adventure at sea, and that the subversive implications of fictions which disturbed even as they consoled were not apparent to contemporary reviewers,[1] just as the projection of an idealistic impulse to imperialism seems to have escaped the anti-imperialist R. B. Cunninghame Graham who read the works as unequivocal assaults on colonialism.[2]

In retrospect and because of radical shifts in historical perspective, altered standards of political morality and new methods of reading, it is now possible to see that the fictions' ironic strategies and alienation techniques do act to redraw the conventional picture of the world, since through demystifying enshrined notions about the unassailable nature of existing social institutions and standards of conduct, the texts confront readers with unacknowledged and discomforting aspects of reality. By transforming the characteristic genres of colonial fiction into vehicles for reflecting on the precepts, values and habits of thought native to these categories, with the narrative material meeting audience expectations and the narrative mediations defamiliarising con-

1

ventional perceptions, disjunctions between the established morality and moral principle are displayed, while ethical absolutes
are revealed to be pragmatic utilities for ensuring social stability
and inhibiting dissent. These innovations from within the forms of
the given mode produce a contrapuntal discourse where the
authentic rendering of imperialism's dominant ideological
categories is undercut by illuminations of the misrecognitions and
limitations in a form of cognition which saw the world in black
and white and admitted only a restricted area of reality to its
purview. Yet, competing with exposures of imperialism's manicheanism and tunnel-vision, there are fantasy representations of
the colonial universe seen across a metaphysical divide which act
to endorse racial solidarity, invite the closing of ethnic ranks, and
confirm western codes as human norms and the ultimate measure
of moral standards.[3]

Critics and commentators who, out of deference for 'genius'
and 'greatness', mute the strident resonances of an author's
reprehensible social stances and intellectually irresponsible
attitudes on the grounds that to discuss these critically is to take
unfair advantage of a contemporary sensibility, make the assumption that all writers are shackled prisoners of dominant modes of
thought. Not only does such an approach obscure the texts'
dimension as 'free intellectual or spiritual production',[4] but it
suppresses articulations that are integral to the fictions' decentred
and internally inconsistent ideological structure. Although Conrad was cool about Kipling, disliked Buchan and thought
Haggard's tales horrible, his own fictions with their racial
stereotypes, ingratiating generalities on alien customs and the
native mind, and their tendency to attach moral valuations to
cultural particularities, do have affinities with writings he
despised. In his works too the East is the consummate figure of the
other: 'perfumed like a flower, silent like death, dark like a grave
. . . so old, so mysterious, resplendent and sombre, living and
unchanged, full of danger and promise . . . where a stealthy
Nemesis lies in wait, pursues, overtakes so many of the conquering race' (*Youth*, (1898) pp. 38, 41, 41–2). Immutable properties
are attributed to the colonial worlds, where the unreconstructed
landscapes transfigure the planet's pre-history and symbolise
moral vacancy, the archaic social arrangements are the extant
form of the primal condition and the peoples personify a state of
stupefied unconsciousness. Confronted by these mythic uni-

verses, their identities realised through negatives – they are inscrutable, immovable, unchanging and old but without a past – the white world gains in stature to stand as the undisputed embodiment of the rational and analytical energies, of human capacity in its evolved form. Within these ethnocentric configurations, the obverse to the disparaging images is the conception of the colonial peoples as possessed of privileged insights into transcendental realms and endowed with magical powers – both the contempt and the awe being in keeping with the conventions of colonial fiction. Where Conrad's writings break with the received perceptions of the other hemisphere as either a metaphysical landscape and/or the incarnation of those desires excluded and repressed by civilisation, is in the dramatisations of the antagonism between western modes and foreign precepts as conflicts of authentic alternatives, and although these invariably issue as victories for the West in the process fundamental questions are asked of European premises and opposing codes are given space to register their claims.

Scholars may differ on defining the source and content of Conrad's double vision, but the consensus is that he is the artist of ambivalence and the divided mind, a writer who discerned and gave novelistic life to those binary oppositions constituting the phylogenetic inheritance of the species and defining its existential condition. That Conrad perceived the world dualistically and was preoccupied by the interaction of antagonistic forces, are propositions abundantly evident in the fictions and confirmed by his commentaries on how he conceived the nature of the fictional undertaking. His essay on Henry James explains his own recourse to warlike images, 'since from the duality of man's nature and the competition of individuals, the life-history of the earth must in the last instance be a history of a really very relentless warfare';[5] and in a letter to the *New York Times* disputing an unfavourable review it had carried of *The Inheritors*, he provocatively affirms a belief in the ubiquity of oppositions:

The only indisputable truth of life is our ignorance. Besides this there is nothing evident, nothing absolute, nothing uncontradicted; there is no principle, no instinct, no impulse that can stand alone at the beginning of things and look confidently to the end . . . The only legitimate basis of creative works lies in the courageous recognition of all the irreconcilable antagonisms that make our life so enigmatic, so burdensome, so fascinating, so dangerous – so full of hope.[6]

It is certain that Conrad's fictions are battle-grounds; however it will be argued that the wars fought can be read as struggles not of metaphysical forces or transhistorical values, but of political doctrines and cultural systems, epistemological suppositions and ontological goals as these are manifest in their historical articulations and forms.

To the extent that the fictions give voice to heterodox values within western traditions and bring the totality of these customs into confrontation with foreign alternatives,[7] they can be interpreted as radically subversive of the official ethos. Within the first category, empiricism is counterposed to scepticism, 'the power to act' to 'the faculty of meditation', 'the fascination of material advantage' to 'the restraint of abstract ideas',[8] triumphalism to inertia, positivism to utopianism. Reason is challenged by unconscious desire and rational cognition by disruptions of 'normal' consciousness, in ways that question and undermine orthodoxies and where the established verities are not necessarily the winners. But when western mores are in conflict with alien structures of experience, the contest is differently articulated and the outcome ideologically determined. Although ethnic solipsism is interrogated and domestic moral axioms deprived of their supremacy, because the other hemisphere *does* represent 'the other', the fictions effectively intercede to decide the contest between two cultures as if these represented two unequal moral universes. Thus even as the fictions rescue from denigration or neglect those notions and goals that are opposed to western norms, the antinomies between the West and Asia/Africa/Latin America, or between North and South, are ultimately transmuted as the antagonism between Ego and Id, Reason and the Irrational, Consciousness and the Unconscious, the Performance Principle and the Pleasure Principle, and in this context the contrary aspirations of instinctual renunciation and gratification, initiative and passivity, innovation and quietism, action and world-negation which were enacted as genuine options within a tradition, become a combat where the values of the white world must assert themselves against the negation of civilisation itself and resist the annihilation of authentic human purpose.

Both disenchanted scrutiny of the flaws to imperialist ways of seeing and complicity in its perceptions are manifest in the contradictory constellations of meaning produced by the fictions' chiaroscuro of light and dark. An obsessive motif in all Conrad's writings where it signifies a multitude of polarities, the iconography of black and white in the colonial novels is integral to the texts' dramatisations of the cultural differences, moral antagonisms and metaphysical antinomies apprehended by the western imagination as structural to the colonial situation. It is a commonplace that in western thought the contrast between black and white has for centuries stood for the good, true, pure and beautiful as opposed to the evil, ignorant, corrupt and atrocious. When the actions of modern imperialism brought the white world into organised confrontations with the other continents, the existing accretions of dark and black were thickened and extended to establish an equivalence between 'primitive', 'barbaric' or 'savage' societies and moral perversity, and by inference between black people living amidst jungle, forest and wilderness and a condition of aboriginal depravity.[9] In Conrad's fictions the dark tropics emanate poisonous influences, decay and death; the sombre, primeval forests whisper of inexplicable desires, the gloomy impenetrable jungles of uncivilised life. However, while such metaphors conform to the authorised image and the fictions go on to develop conventional western connotations, the texts also invert customary usage, a reversal which calls into question the received values of a social order inordinately boastful of its own excellence. If Conrad does use white and light as the signs of truth, integrity, knowledge, decency and reason, he also annuls these associations when the conspicuous objects of imperialist desire, the gold of *Almayer's Folly*, the ivory of *Heart of Darkness* and the silver of *Nostromo*, serve as emblems of avarice and agents of corruption. Conversely, while black does signify evil, death, hell, chaos and moral nullity, it is also the figure of transcendent reality and ultimate meanings, overarching the facile and transparent truths visible in the light. Nor is Conrad's dark a monolith: like a blanket it can blind and suffocate, but it can also reach the eye as luminous and meet the touch as velvet.[10]

The history of Conrad criticism is the history of changing methods and concerns in contemporary literary studies, and abstracts of the vast literature about his fiction display the presence of every stance in the critical canon. A closer look at this body of expository

writing will show that while work on Conrad's intellectual
heritage, political ideas and historical imagination continues to be
produced,[11] the predominant trend has been away from discussing what has been termed the 'public dimensions' and towards
analysing the novels as either ontological meditations and
psychological explorations, or as symbolic representations of
'transhistorical' realities.[12] The hazards both in empiricist readings of self-evidently historical texts and in formalist procedures
that suppress their immanent political meanings are apparent.
Just as commentaries preoccupied with identifying sources,
origins and factual equivalences do not engage with the fictiveness
of the writings, so do the paradigms of metaphysical, ethical or
allegorical worlds conferred by critics seeking to establish the
existence of universal and invariable categories remain dissociated from the historically produced ideology which the fictions
signify, criticise and augment. To bring political criticism to
Conrad's writings is not to isolate the 'sociologically significant'
aspects of the novels, nor to initiate a survey of their historical
authenticity, realistic features or tendentious design, and indeed
the primary concern of such analysis is to understand the
relationships between literature and history at the level of a
work's formal, literary structures.

Fictions that both in their own day and subsequently contributed to the making of western opinion about late nineteenth-
century imperialism and the worlds it conquered, and which
because of past interpretative intercessions were handed down as
valid testimony about those times and places, have inevitably
invoked dissertations on the relationship between this specific
historical context and the history intrinsic to Conrad's 'colonial
novels', and impinging on the general enquiry are variously
conceived researches situated in the more specialised area
concerned with the literary subculture of imperialism.[13] By the
very nature of its terms, this undertaking is in danger of reading
the fictions as 'reflections' of an objective reality or as 'mediations'
of prevalent political attitudes and cultural values, a tendency
which points up the endemic problems in the debate on fiction
and society or history. Although the high incidence of
methodological lapses in the study of literature and imperialism
should not be taken as evidence of an intrinsically disabling factor
invalidating the discussion itself, it should serve to caution critics
against using fiction as a form of writing aspiring to replicate,

explain and normalise the lineaments of the real world, a procedure which would yield reductive interpretations of the texts and singularly unreliable empirical evidence about history.

If, however, literature is approached as an autonomous practice producing specifically fictional representations of what has through other means been construed as history, then criticism can elucidate the texts' eccentric perceptions of the epistemological premises, ethical axioms and social goals proposed by the dominant ideology, and this study will attempt to discuss how the interlocution of narrative discourses in a set of Conrad's fictions transforms, subverts and rescues the established norms, values and myths of imperialist civilisation. For within Conrad's writings the animations of received ideas, beliefs and apprehensions that act to ratify the *status quo* engender a protest against the authorised sources as these are dislocated and distorted to make the normal appear strange, to reveal the fixed as mutable and expose the absolute as relative. It is the presence of incommensurable meanings, which are articulated in the dialogue of voices soliciting support for antithetical ideas and principles, and generated by the discontinuities between what the action shows and what the narrative says, between the fiction's indwelling significations and the formal constructions imposed by narrative exegesis and rhetoric, that displays the text's struggle to escape ideology and the pressures drawing it back into the orbit of the imperialist world-view.

Imperialism is necessarily a controversial word since it has been used and sometimes abused by competing bodies of ideas to describe a diversity of unrelated historical developments. Although repudiated by some academics as a term unfit for scholars, it has always been central to the Marxist vocabulary and is now widely accepted as necessary to understanding those processes which have defined the structure of the modern world and continue to characterise its interrelationships. Those historians and economists concerned with formulating a coherent theory of imperialism have acknowledged that the undertaking is beset by conceptual ambiguity and terminological confusion:

Marxists since Lenin have in fact fluctuated in their use of the term imperialism. Very often it has been used to describe the whole capitalist system; just as often it refers to the relations between advanced and backward countries within the system.

Sometimes it is used in both senses simultaneously, either with or more often without, an acknowledgement of the ambiguity involved.[14]

Because the essence of modern imperialism is the formation of a world economic system generated by the impulses of western capitalism and dominated by its needs, its usage cannot be confined to colonialism, a particular mode within its many and mutable states, and one which preceded the growth of international finance capital and whose formal ending imperialism survived. But when it is applied exclusively to the changing forms of capitalism and the concomitant transformations in social relationships and traditional values within the metropolitan society, then the effect is to relegate the West's conquest of the 'third world' to a contingent status and occlude the system of global domination exercised by the white nations as a necessary outgrowth of capitalism and its most spectacular export.

A Eurocentric orientation to the discussion has been disputed by participants who point out that the contributions made by imperialism's 'consumers or victims'[15] are concentrated on defining the material conditions, social relationships, patterns of conflict and ideological premises specific to those colonial situations produced by the invasions of modern imperialism, incursions which disrupted existing societies and delimited the future possibilities of whole continents. The arguments of this controversy have influenced the political interpretations of literary texts, and to claim as one critic has done that Conrad's 'colonial' fictions' before *Nostromo* signally fail to confront the nature and dynamics of imperialism as a system,[16] is to circumscribe the inherent significations of the concept and truncate the compass of Conrad's historical imagination. For if Conrad did not see imperialism steadily, he did, in fictions that dramatise the war of the hemispheres within a structurally joined and spiritually divided universe, see it whole, thereby inviting readers to scrutinise the ethical foundations to the civilisation of expansionist capitalism and engaging them in a critical view of imperialism's urge to conquer the earth.

The same ambiguity that attaches to the use of imperialism applies also to the properties of imperialism's dominant ideology. In its general sense this ideology[17] can be understood as the system of representations produced by established institutions through which individuals living their roles within the class structure of late capitalism learn to assimilate their existing positions and relationships as natural, permanent and conforming to a transcendent ethical plan. When used more specifically, imperialist ideology can be taken to mean that constellation of values, beliefs and myths giving intellectual coherence and moral sanction to colonialism (the burden of a racial and national mission, service to a noble corporate cause, implementation of the laws of order and progress in the dark places of the earth), which foster in men and women a form of cognition whereby they come to identify themselves as members of a ruling race, identify with the conception of a great national destiny and accede to the relationship of power and dominance between the West and other continents. Although this study is principally concerned with the latter meaning, this is conceived as integral to the larger ideology, which in the epoch of colonial expansion acted to undermine the class consciousness generated by socialism with appeals to the supreme authority of a patriotism that an historian has described as being 'above class, loyal to the institutions of the country, and resolute in defence of its honour and interests'.[18]

To explain and justify the West's galactic ambitions and establish its title to global paramountcy, imperialism's propagandists devised the heady conceit of Europe's messianic destiny as the saviour of benighted peoples, asserted as proven the existence of a master race and represented the species' interactive relationship with its material conditions as one demanding total control of the physical environment. Raymond Williams has described the 'triumphalist version of "man's conquest of nature" ' as a theory that is 'in an exceptionally close correspondence, the specific ideology of imperialism and capitalism, whose basic concepts – limitless and conquering expansion; reduction of the labour process to the appropriation and transformation of raw materials – it exactly repeats';[19] and the apprehension of this corporate will to domination and supremacy is central to Conrad's perception of imperialism's inspiration and aspiration. Within the many ideological forms coexisting in the age of imperialist expansion, it was an assemblage fusing pragmatism and irrationalism, utilitarianism and metaphysics in a noxious conflation, and that was definitively configured in Cecil John Rhodes's dream of annexing the planets, which Conrad's fictions illuminate and interrogate – the temperament of a puritan joined with an 'insatiable imagination of conquest', 'the misty idealism of the Northerners, who at the smallest encouragement dream of nothing less than the conquest of the earth' (*Nostromo*, pp. 76, 333).

The retrospect on modern imperialism presents special problems to western critics living within or on the periphery of an intellectual environment where the old colonial lore has retained the power to elicit nostalgia for the horizons empire once spanned and lost, the passing of the privileged life of service and romance is still regretted and new legends legitimising both past exploits and contemporary neo-imperialist interventions are being newly devised.[20] Because of this continuous process of rehabilitation, even those critics who deplore the many unlovely entries in imperialism's annals can in their readings of the literary texts display an attenuated apprehension of imperialism's apocalyptic urges (which if exercised by a western nation on peer nations would have inspired a holy war against the anti-christ daring to pursue such an ambition) and express a remote disavowal of the insult and injury inflicted on foreign populations in the fulfilment of these impulses. Thus a convulsive process which radically altered the organisation of metropolitan societies and disintegrated the existing social orders of the conquered land, is represented as a stage in an inevitable and necessary progress devised by a benign but determined meta-intelligence, in the course of which some unkindness and injustice has inadvertently been committed. In critical discussion of Conrad's work, this bland approach which sterilises the theory and obfuscates the practice of imperialism acts to mute and even suppress the fictions' negative representations of the imperialist vocation. For by revealing the disjunctions between high-sounding rhetoric and sordid ambitions and indicting the purposes and goals of a civilisation dedicated to global expansionism and hegemony, Conrad's writings engender a critique more destructive of imperialism's ideological premises than do the polemics of his contemporary opponents of empire.

But while the fictions can be seen to sabotage the mystique of empire through refusing the received account as mendacious, to read these works as univocal denunciations of imperialist mores, motives and dreams is to overlook those textual processes which not only leave imperialist assumptions intact but originate perceptions of a latent idealism indwelling in what was manifestly a soulless project. The interaction of these discontinuous meanings within the text makes it inappropriate to discuss the fictions' transformations of imperialist ideology within a conceptual framework contained by a critic/apologist dichotomy, since neither the repudiations nor the vindications conform to the terms of reference used in arguments against and for imperialism. On the one hand the censure, which moves between the poles of social concern and moral testament, exceeds the boundaries of political debate and on the other, the affirmation of saving ideas postulates heterodox motives and ends at variance with imperialism's declared and covert ambitions. That the proferring of a visionary dimension to imperialism was doomed to fail was an irony that did not escape Conrad in his many meditations on the wasting of utopian desire when attached to pragmatic purposes and immoral goals. All the same, the effect of seeking to recover the spiritual forces at work or incipient in imperialism is to arrest the reappraisal of beliefs demanded by the fiction's arguments and revelations, even as it stands as a sign of the principle of hope.

If imperialism's terms of seeing are confuted by the texts, they are also restored through being rewritten in forms more acceptable to advocates of moral conscience, where they serve to prolong the life of disreputable justifications and vindicate the sophistries of an extravagantly mystified rationale. But since the ethos of the existing system has been discredited and cannot be exonerated, alternative bases for allegiance are insinuated by appeals to ethnic solidarity and protestations of the spiritual value inhering in patriotism that ask no questions of the principles to which the race is dedicated or the goals to which the nation aspires. With the intercession of this discourse, the texts themselves become accomplices in the life-lie necessary to the existence of a world that can neither be defended nor disavowed, and as moral authority is restored to a civilisation which has been exposed to be in a state of moral disarray, the fictions' stark representation of imperialism as the very figure of a ruthless triumphalism is clothed in veils of sentiment and idealism. Ironically it was a minor collaborative work, *The Inheritors* (1901), a political fantasy written with Ford Maddox Hueffner/Ford (and which he felt called upon to defend from hostile reviewers although his own part in the writing had been small) that Conrad, in a passage to which he certainly contributed even if the cadences are not characteristically his, registered an unequivocal protest against the absolute depen-

dence of imperialist Europe on institutionalised deception. Here
the weak but decent protagonist, appalled by disclosures about a
continental imperialist venture in which Britain is deeply implicated, is driven to acknowledge the official inspiration as meretricious and the moral sanctions sustaining his country's social
system as mendacious:

> There were revolting details of cruelty to the miserable,
> helpless, and defenceless; there were greed, and self-seeking,
> stripped naked; but more revolting to see without a mask was
> that falsehood which had been hiding under the words that for
> ages had spurred men to noble deeds, to self-sacrifice, to
> heroism. What was appalling was the sudden perception that
> all the traditional ideals of honour, glory, conscience, had been
> committed to the upholding of a gigantic and atrocious fraud.
> The falsehood had spread stealthily, had eaten into the very
> hearts of creeds and convictions that we lean upon in our
> passages between the past and the future. The old order of
> things had to live or perish with a lie. (pp. 184–5)

The intellectual and ethical ambiguities embraced by Conrad's
colonial fictions have deeper sources and take more paradoxical
forms that can be suggested by locating his casuistry in excluding
Britain's colonial ventures from the general castigation of
imperialist exploits, or by referring to a letter he wrote to a Polish
relative where he states that liberty 'can only be found under the
English flag all over the world'[21] – both unsatisfactory illustra-
tions of his double-think since those fictions which formally
propose that good work is being done in the red places of the map
also negate the exemption. Nor can his much-quoted letter
scorning 'the criminality of inefficiency and pure selfishness when
tackling the civilising work in Africa'[22] be taken as the felt
statement of one who despised the method but approved the
mission, for when repeated in the fictions the very notion of
'civilising work' is derided as colonialist cant. Alone amongst
novelists writing at the turn of the century, Conrad perceived
theoretical imperialism to be a dissimulation of the conditions and
relationships it purported to explain, a view animated in fictions
where protagonists are exposed to situations revealing that the
system of beliefs by which they live, and which inspire them to
fulfil their social obligations, is an elaborate system of misrepre-

sentations. Conrad's hostile perspective on imperialism was influenced by the views of his friend R. B. Cunninghame Graham, who in his many anti-imperialist writings attacked a corrupted social-darwinism justifying territorial acquisition on the grounds of superior material strength and equating such power with moral superiority, castigated colonialism for demeaning the civilisations of both coloniser and colonised, and maintained that the attempt to found a durable and decent moral order on the basis of material interests was doomed.[23]

However, Conrad's own composite and inconsistent outlook inhibited concurrence with any of the current postures, and neither the chauvinism of the imperialists, the internationalism of the radical anti-imperialists nor the liberal position which deplored colonial brutalities while energetically or apologetically endorsing the project as materially necessary to both hemispheres as well as morally advantageous to the colonised, were congenial to him. The theories produced by the ideologues of late nineteenth-century imperialism had ostensibly succeeded in reconciling a formal commitment to humanitarianism and the inviolability of national integrity with the aggressive pursuit of profit and political advantage in distant lands where the code of humane values was suspended and notions of territorial sovereignty violated. Fundamental to a construction defending imperialism's formal goals as ethical and its practices as globally beneficial, and one which was accepted by large numbers within the metropolitan society as an accurate apprehension of realities and conforming to sound principle, were the premises that civilisation was defined by an expanding technology, progress by the increased domination of the material environment, culture by the tastes of the European bourgeosie and morality by Christian doctrine. The terms of this internally coherent but factitious explanation, based on the ruling-class interests of a dominant nation, were repugnant to Conrad, who continued to identify himself as belonging to the dispossessed Polish gentry, was wedded to the chivalric codes of his ancestral tradition and disdainful of middle-class materialism, was out of sympathy with British pragmatism, alienated from institutionalised Christianity, uneasy about foreign rule over subjugated peoples, and offended by the vulgar and self-congratulatory jingoism which flourished in the age of colonial expansion.[24]

All the same, if the émigré Pole was distanced from the ways in which his peers in England experienced their world, and looked on the moral axioms of imperialism as social utilities, then Britain was the place of exile chosen by Conrad in his flight from the political upheavals of his homeland and the disintegration of his family life, which indicates that there were facets of England's social order and its prevalent ways of seeing that were congenial to him.[25] Born into a landowning family whose members had been associated with both the militant and moderate wings of Polish nationalism, Conrad belonged to a community which was politically and culturally dominated by Russia and Prussia and in turn exercised dominion over their Ukranian serfs, making them as Avrom Fleishman (op. cit.) has pointed out, a group that was not only colonised but also colonialist. This situation exposed him to conditions known by both parties to the imperialist confrontation; however Conrad, who insisted that Poland was an outpost of westernism and fiercely affirmed his identity as a European, was eloquent about Poland's sufferings as a civilised nation of high moral calibre persecuted by barbarians and tyrants, while justifying its own earlier annexations on the grounds of cultural superiority[26] – a dubious argument which he did not extend to the West's colonial conquests. When the expatriate patriot felt called upon to express his support for preserving the 'national spirit' against the debilitating effects of international fraternity,[27] made it known that he found revolutionary ideas repugnant and dissociated himself from the 'subversion of any social or political scheme of existence',[28] he was speaking in tones that had affinities with the ruling-class voice of his adopted country which suggests that his estrangement from England was moderated by a deep sympathy for its conservative mores.[29]

It has been argued that the origins and articulations of Conrad's adherence to established institutions situate his posture outside the mainstream of nineteenth-century political conservatism. Z. Najder traces such views to conditions in Poland where the movement to restore the integrity of the partitioned homeland was inseparable from the defence of traditionalism: 'His was the outlook of the uprooted nobleman. The values he wanted to see cherished – honour, duty, fidelity, friendship – were typically romantic and typically chivalrous.'[30] Avrom Fleishman, however, connects Conrad's commendation of the work ethic and his ideal of the highly integrated and cohesive human collective to the tradition of Victorian organicism which rejected contemporary

liberal-individualism and invoked extinct forms of social organisation. It is true that, in his search to discover redemptive
features in the imperialist idea, Conrad did turn back to past
ideologies and it was in the old values of two diverse but
complementary European traditions, the one undermined by the
flourishing of competitive individualism, the other made redun-
dant by the organised colonialist ventures of the powerful
capitalist nations, both moribund when resuscitated by imperialism's propaganda to inspire and mobilise its agents, that Conrad
sought to locate its positive impulses. On the one hand he
recreated as a significant social order the closely knit and
hierarchical community bound together by obedience to fixed
standards of conduct and belief in work as an ascetic discipline, a
form of organisation incarnate for him in the merchant navy,[31]
and one that had been adopted as the ideal of the British Service
Classes in the age of colonial rule. On the other hand, in the
frequent acclamations of the disinterested, intrepid and honourable pioneers who, by opening up territory to western penetration, were the unconscious bearers of Culture and Coherence into
the realm of Nature and Chaos, he drew on and enhanced the
mythology of a brave and beneficent colonialism. Conrad may in
his essays have dismissed 'adventure' as futile and reserved his
praise for 'service',[32] but in the fictions both the mythic past and
extant remnants of an archaic practice are extolled as manifestations of imperialism's saving virtues. However, at this
juncture it becomes apparent that the impulse behind the search
for a positive dimension to imperialism emanates not from
nostalgia for a bygone age, not from the wish to recover an Edenic
condition or to glorify the history of colonial ventures, but from
the utopian urge to transfigure still unrealised ideals. It is this
transposition of the dreams of tomorrow to distant yesterdays
which causes the horizons of the past to be emptied of heroes for
the visionary expectations of historically located protagonists
whose autonomy is curtailed by their roles as agents of imperialist's purpose, who are doomed to deformation and defeat.

Still the problem remains of interpreting the implications to the
plaudits bestowed by the fictions on the work-ethic, service and
action where no ends are specified, since these affirmations in the
texts issue as endorsements of loyalty to the existing system, just
as the doctrines of ethnic solidarity and reverence for the national
spirit that takes no account of the objects to which the race and

the nation are committed culminate in celebrations of a patriotism and act as an ideological support of the imperialist system.
This is in no way to suggest that Conrad's fictions can be
construed as manifestoes of the imperialist vocation and memori-
als to its exalted aspiration, for by locating the model of the
authentic human community in a body that was undeniably an
instrument of colonial trade and policy and therefore party to
imperialist conquest, Conrad makes space for history to penetrate
the texts and destroy the pretensions of the abstract idea; while by
attempting to chronicle the lives of colonisers as Promethean
figures, he is obliged to show them to be fallible adventurers or
impersonators of imperialism's aggressive and engorging will.
Thus in the very act of seeking valorisation for imperialism, the
fictions are forced to acknowledge compelling disproof of the
theories advanced, and the urge to recover the imperialist myth
and nurture it as irreplaceable is overcome by the perception that
it is indefensible. Yet from within overtly bleak and expressly
disenchanted fictions signs of promise are generated, and here the
writer who in his public utterances castigated pessimists and
insisted on the need to cherish undying hope,[33] remained
paradoxically true to his own prescriptions. Ironically and
unexpectedly the symbols of anticipation inhere in experiences
and desires disparaged by the texts – in the many auguries of a
fuller and more extensive human condition prefigured in
moments of ontological awakening which are formally denigrated
and luminously realised – and in *Nostromo*, the one novel standing
as Conrad's fullest engagement with the meanings and values of
imperialist civilisation, in nervous intimations of a far horizon
that, against the grain of its formal intentions, irradiates the
fiction as the goal of the mistrusted and traduced millenarian
faith.

The variety of titles listed in the bibliographies of the critical
literature on Conrad[34] suggests the old and characteristic Jewish
story about the treatise of an earnest zoologist and concerned Jew
on The Elephant and the Jewish Question; everything in the
cornucopia of ideas has been deemed relevant to Conrad's
writings just as his fictions have been made to impinge on virtually
all problems relating to human existence. So energetically have
affinities with the major and heterogenous intellectual and
literary tendencies of his age been claimed, that one scholar was

driven to accuse contemporary criticism of casting Conrad in an 'absurd number of more or less incompatible roles: as an impressionist, as a *symboliste* of sorts, as an allegorist (Jungian or Freudian) and more recently as a political moralist of reactionary, conservative, organicist, existentialist or even revolutionary tendencies'.[35] If this magisterial rebuke is indiscriminate in deriding fanciful conjectures that float ethereally above the texts as well as interpretations that do engage with the fictions' overt and concealed meanings, it does draw attention to the self-indulgence of Conrad criticism that cumulatively has made of its subject a man for all seasons and an exemplar or precursor of every conceivable fictional mode and philosophical tradition. What it overlooks is that the diversity of the expository offerings is itself engendered by the text's multivalencies, for as Fredric Jameson has shown, 'the discontinuities objectively present in Conrad's narratives, have, as with few other modern writers, projected a bewildering variety of competing and incommensurable interpretative options' (*The Political Unconscious*, p. 208).

Monuments honouring his stature continue to be built and the two majestic edifices erected in recent years by Frederick Karl[36] and Ian Watt[37] may make smaller and differently designed constructions appear insignificant if not superfluous. Indeed it was Professor Karl who on another occasion reproved critics for the volume and quality of their output and recommended a moratorium on further studies devoted to a writer 'about whom very little remains to be said unless as a result of original scholarship, manuscripts and typescripts, comparative readings of revisions of texts, unpublished letters, hitherto unexamined relations with other writers or with compelling issues of the period'.[38] But neither this proposal of a self-denying ordinance for critics derived from a narrow notion of critical practice, nor Professor Watt's courteous attempt to promote a consensus amongst diverse and indeed irreconcilable opinions on the meanings of Conrad's texts, will inhibit the hermeneutical process. Readers, whether lay or professional, will because of their particular situations in a changing society, their relationships to shifts in historical perspective and their participation in innovative ways of reading, perceive the fictions anew and will continue to bring original interpretations to them, constructing the texts within changing ideological parameters, recognising hitherto unnoticed allusions, listening with differently attuned ears to their resonances and dissonances. The proposition that there exists one correct reading which it is the critical task to elucidate, is blatantly called into question by the discrepant discoveries made in Conrad's colonial fictions by practised readers. For V. S. Naipaul, who shares Conrad's perception of the West as the embodiment of reason if not his moral indignation at imperialism's legacy to the colonised, Conrad's writings project an authentic vision of the world's half-made, fragile and unfinished societies, of the earth's dark places with their empty landscapes devoid of the human, with no history and no past.[39] They can also be received as the fantasies of a nineteenth-century European imagination which retain the power to insult present-day audiences in the third world[40] and to shock those in the West who are estranged from the racist assumptions of the past and refuse the solace of retroactive justifications.

The ways in which a fiction can be interpreted are not unlimited since the process of reception is constrained by the content of the empirical text, but the creative role of the reader in responding to writings whose meanings are not fixed for all times remains a crucial factor in literary analysis. This is a proposition of which Conrad would have approved:

> No secret of eternal life for our books can be found amongst the formulas of art, any more than for our bodies in a prescribed combination of drugs. This is not because some books are not worthy of enduring life, but because the formulas of art are dependent on things variable, unstable and untrustworthy; on human sympathies, on prejudices, on likes and dislikes, on the sense of virtue and the sense of propriety, on beliefs and theories that, indestructible in themselves, always change their form.[41]

It is this potentiality for continuous reincarnation through the intercessions of critical discussion which assures life to the products of past cultural milieux, without which the fictions of bygone ages would be consigned to the vaults of the measureless unread. This finally is the apology for yet another study on Conrad.

> Now he is scattered among a hundred cities
> And wholly given over to unfamiliar affections,
> To find his happiness in another kind of wood

And be punished under a foreign code of conscience.
The words of a dead man
Are modified in the guts of the living.

W. H. Auden: 'In Memory of W. B. Yeats' (1939), *Collected Poems* (London: Faber and Faber, 1976, p. 197)

2 *Heart of Darkness*

A fiction which develops contradictory representations and condenses incompatible positions will speak in different voices to its readers,[1] and these include the professional critics who, in the vast literature generated by this novella, have brought diverse systems of meaning to explain its multivalencies.[2] *Heart of Darkness* registers its manifold preoccupations in a title which by signifying a geographical location, a metaphysical landscape and a theological category, addresses itself simultaneously to Europe's exploitation of Africa, the primeval human situation, an archaic aspect of the mind's structure and a condition of moral baseness. The rich possibilities for critical speculation are apparent and amongst the many readings advanced, the book has been interpreted as an attack on imperialism, a parable about the construction of ethical values, a mythic descent into the primal underworld, a night journey into the unconscious self and a spiritual voyage towards transcendent knowledge. The presupposition to the present discussion is that in joining an allegory about the destiny of colonialism's meretricious aspiration with a mythopoeic narration of the West's penetration into the estranging world of its other, the fiction paradoxically contains within itself the seeds of an unorthodox apologia for values it has discredited and disowned.

Because of a decentred structure, *Heart of Darkness* produces a critical reflection on the very forms of consciousness it illuminates and a critique of an ethos that is ultimately undermined by a discourse invoking solidarity with the progenitors of a system based on and sustained by lies, and the concern here will be to distinguish the distancing procedures Conrad used to disturb habitual responses from those strategies calculated to invite adherence to the existing order. If Conrad's much-quoted remark to his publisher that 'The criminality of inefficiency and pure selfishness when tackling the civilising work in Africa is a justifiable idea'[3] suggests equivocal attitudes towards colonial-

20

ism, then the development of the idea produces a fiction that faces in opposite directions, denouncing as infamous the assumptions underpinning imperialism's formal ideology while producing for its canon the vindication of idealistic intent. Whereas estranging devices make space for a discussion that animates imperialism as a state of social disorder and moral breakdown, and discloses its rationale to be a fantasy account of circumstances to which it bears an inverse relationship, other discourses, endorsing customary ways of seeing together with constellations of images congenial to the dominant consciousness, coalesce in producing a view of the world that conforms to colonialist theology. Nor is repudiation of the West's colonialist ambitions the fiction's final or most reverberatory words, and with the supervention of themes registering ethical standards as fixed by ethnic sentiment and servering acts of personal honour from a wider conception of moral responsibility, the political protest is crucially muffled and the grace of visionary aspirations invested in imperialism triumphs over representations of the disgrace attending its historical practice.

The manicheanism of the imperialist imagination which perceived a world of warring moral forces, incompatible social modes and antagonistic values, is registered and interrogated in the fiction's insistently dichotomous iconography. Asserting itself over the variegated and specific colours of images evoking the vibrant tones of the jungle or particularising the hues of a map, flames, a motley outfit, and striped draperies, is the commanding motif of white and black, the luminous and the sombre, light and dark. Domino pieces, a keyboard, an altercation between an African and a European over two black hens, a Belgian woman clothed in black, wearing a white head-dress and knitting black wool, white surf edging a black jungle, a black moustache on a white face, dark eyes in a pale face, white eyeballs in a black face, a piece of white worsted tied around a black neck, shrunken black heads with white teeth, Kurtz's ivory pate and the bronze bodies of his devotees – these figurations compose a chiaroscuro which while innocently reproducing a basic perceptual distinction and neutrally signifying the prevalence of dualities, more consequentially maps the landscape of the imperialist mind.[4] By investing the paired opposites with those meanings and values long conventionalised within the western consciousness, the fiction reveals a fundamental tenet of colonialist mythology where white

and black are unambiguously emblematic of good and evil, truth
and ignorance, the chaste and the defiled: Kurtz's Intended is a
'soul as pure as a cliff of crystal', her fair hair and white brow the
visible signs of her capacity for fidelity, belief and trust; the dark
jungle is hopeless and impenetrable to human thought; the
beastly night strikes one sightless; Kurtz, 'a shadow darker than
the shadow of night', is prey to the powers of darkness; Africa,
where there are no restraints to brutal instincts and monstrous
passions, exists in the night of first ages. In this contrast moral
antitheses are lodged: for Marlow the 'pure uncomplicated
savagery' of African life is 'something that had a right to exist –
obviously – in the sunshine', whereas Kurtz's depravities had
transported him into 'some lightless region of subtle horrors'
(p. 132) – a multifaceted image which uses received notions joining simplicity to light and decadence to darkness, and disturbs
expectations by allotting the Africans a place in the sunshine and
consigning the white man to the shades. Confused by reports of
Kurtz's gorgeous eloquence, Marlow ponders on 'the gift of
expression, the bewildering, the illuminating, the most exalted
and the most contemptible, the pulsating stream of light, or the
deceitful flow from the heart of an impenetrable darkness'
(pp. 113–14).

The iconography is, however, altogether more ambivalent than
such usage would suggest since the antinomian categories are
subjected to a radical rearrangement subverting Europe's customary imagery, so that instead of denoting purity, virtue, clarity
and veracity, white and light – which can be lurid as well as
tranquil – come to signify corruption, evil, confusion and lies. The
clean white city of Brussels which for Marlow resembles a whited
sepulchre, is the place from where a rapacious colonialism is
organised; the eyes of a venal agent in the Congo glitter like mica
discs; the object of European cupidity and veneration, and the
means whereby the invaders are themselves held captive is the
ivory. The whiteness of a marble fireplace is cold and forbidding;
white fog is more blinding than the night and sunlight can be
made to lie; the pale and ethereal Intended lives by a delusion;
Kurtz's sketch of a blindfolded woman posed against a black
background and carrying a torch that casts a sinister light on her
face transforms Europe's traditional figure of justice into an image
of that continent's arrogant, unseeing and unjust invasion of
Africa. An immediate consequence of reversing the received

associations is that the moral categories defining the western sensibility are disarrayed and the myopic bias of colonialist consciousness revealed;[5] the more profound effect is that Europe is deposed from its self-elevation as harbinger of light in a dark continent.

However, although the resonances of white are rendered discordant, those of black are not made harmonious, since black and dark do serve in the text as equivalences for the savage and unredeemed, the corrupt and degraded, the abominable and the detestable, the cruel and atrocious. Imperialism itself is perceived as the dark within Europe, invading the house of Kurtz's Intended, swathing the biggest and the greatest town on earth in mournful gloom, shrouding the tranquil waters of the Thames, its ominous shadow reaching to the ends of the earth. But other meanings too are conferred on black and images of the dark transfigure both the incomprehensible and the uncomprehended, the malignant and the majestic, not only Kurtz's descent into an 'impenetrable darkness' but his enlightenment and moral victory, so that Marlow recalling his own subsequent contest with death as taking place in an 'impalpable greyness . . . without form' celebrates in Kurtz's last moments a passage through the dark to ultimate knowledge: 'his stare, that could not see the flame of the candle, but was wide enough to embrace the whole universe, piercing enough to penetrate all the hearts that beat in the darkness' (p. 151). Marlow's ambiguous justification for withholding from the Intended the story of Kurtz's life and death in Africa because 'it would have been too dark – too dark altogether', implies both the abnormal content of what he gallantly conceals and his conviction that a woman of her breeding and temperament would be incapable of assimilating profound truths. Black and dark do then signify positive qualities; moreover they come to portend absolutes: immanent in Africa's dark wilderness are 'overwhelming realities' and 'invincible truths' inaccessible to empiricist modes of cognition and outside the narrow range of experience ratified by western cultures. Yet despite such momentous departures from traditional European usage which serve to question imperialism's informing suppositions and disclose its misrecognitions, the fiction gravitates back to established practice, registering the view of two incompatible orders within a manichean universe, and by this obliquely conferring a specious righteousness on an otherwise indefensible ethnic allegiance.

It is evident that the techniques of *Heart of Darkness* have been devised as if by a producer who in assembling his drama has eschewed depicting familiar subjects as natural and normal: the landscape is mythic, the scenery surreal, the circumstances grotesque, the peripheral characters iconic and the oratorical delivery of the protagonists remote from ordinary speech.[6] Readers acquainted with colonialism's doctrines and the official version of its aspiration and practice are thus invited to make new and conscious judgements of received assumptions and reported conditions because these have been transmuted as strange and astonishing.[7] In devising an imperialist situation that is insane and nightmarish, fantastic and ludicrous, a 'sordid farce acted in front of a sinister back-cloth' (p. 61), the fiction shows that imperialism's norms and standards are bizarre, and since the avatar of its material ambitions and moral purpose is a man whose surplus gratification of colonialist desires had culminated in the transgression of European mores, the imperialist project is stripped of its mystique as the divinely ordained and historically determined agency of bringing the earth under rational rule. The patent artifice of the script and the mannered acting styles of protagonists who are used as communicating intelligences but whose insights prove unreliable, whose beliefs emerge as unsound and whose words belie their conduct, is calculated to deter readers from automatically regarding any of the viewpoints advanced as authoritative. Thus Marlow occupies the centre of the stage with a practised narrative delivered in the language of a metroplis while reiterating a mistrust of words,[8] affirming the eloquence of gestures and cries and pointing back to the silent wilderness as the repository of transcendent truth and ultimate reality.

The opening address of the primary narrator, spoken in a voice that is alternately bluff, ingratiating and oracular, can appear to be a portentous extolment of Britain's imperial might and the glory of its colonial endeavours:

> And indeed nothing is easier for a man who has, as the phrase goes, 'followed the sea' with reverence and affection, than to evoke the great spirit of the past upon the lower reaches of the Thames . . . It had known and served all the men of whom the nation is proud, from Sir Francis Drake to Sir John Franklin, knights all, titled and untitled – the great knights-errant of the sea. It had borne all the ships whose names are like jewels

flashing in the night of time, from the *Golden Hind* returning
with her round flanks full of treasure . . . to the *Erebus* and
Terror, bound on other conquests – and that never returned. It
had known the ships and the men . . . Hunters for gold or
pursuers of fame, they had all gone out on that stream, bearing
the sword, and often the torch, messengers of the might within
the land, bearers of a spark from the sacred fire. What greatness
had not floated on the ebb of that river into the mystery of an
unknown earth! – The dreams of men, the seed of common-
wealths, the germs of empires. (p. 47)

Since each phrase of this ostensible tribute, in which recognition
of mercenary motives is offset by praise for visionary impulses, is
to be annulled by the fiction's action, these remarks necessarily
serve as an object of irony, especially as the speaker with apparent
innocence makes known that he and his companions, who are
Marlow's audience, are all connected with 'overseas trade'.
However, the imagist manner of his presentation, with its
dualistic motifs, metonyms of menace and contrapuntal structure
where every expression of positive sentiment is nullified by its
opposite, is at odds with the conventions of celebratory rhetoric
and makes the speaker an active communicator of irony whose
very words carry the seeds of their own subversion. Nor is his style
consistent since he exceeds his role as the chorus who delivers the
prologue and provides elliptical commentary, by communicating
his sensitivity to the pervasive disquiet of Marlow's tale and in a
spare and bleak epilogue lacking the sonorities and negating the
ambivalent affirmations of the opening remarks that formally
stand as his final retrospect, making known his own education.

All the same, his few, brief intercessions do operate equivocally
within a text which confirms some of his pronouncements while
invalidating others. It is his metaphor distinguishing Marlow's
delivery from the direct simplicity of the usual seafarer's yarn
which defines the fiction's narrative structure within which the
forms of a colonial adventure story are used and superseded to
register a critical judgement on its conventions and inscribed
morality: 'to him the meaning of an episode was not inside like a
kernel but outside, enveloping the tale which brought it out only
as a glow brings out a haze, in the likeness of one of those misty
halos that sometimes are made visible by the spectral illumination
of moonshine' (p. 48). On the other hand, his testimony on

Marlow as a guru is unsupported by Marlow's insistence on his partial knowledge and imperfect understanding, his groping a way towards comprehending events into which he had been drawn:

> It was the farthest point of navigation and the culminating point of my experience. It seemed somehow to throw a kind of light on everything about me – and into my thoughts. It was sombre enough, too – and pitiful – not extraordinary in any way – not very clear either. No, not very clear. And yet it seemed to throw a kind of light. (p. 51)

Just as the speech of the anonymous first narrator discredits the authority of the opinions he advances, so does Marlow's narration draw attention to the lacunae and inconsistencies in his own outlook. Marlow's advocacy of the work code[9] has the conviction of one who has indeed found his 'own reality' through approaching any given task with the 'enthusiasm of a connoisseur' and discharging it with the care and dedication of a craftsman. For him an unadorned manual on seamanship is made 'luminous with another than a professional light' because of 'a singleness of intention, an honest concern for the right way of going to work' (p. 99), and his contempt for the band of sordid buccaneers calling themselves the Eldorado Exploring Expedition is directed at their debasement of such standards: 'there was not an atom of foresight or of serious intention in the whole batch of them, and they did not seem aware that these things are wanted for the work of the world' (p. 87). It is a creed that posits an ethic of responsibility without specifying the goal such devotion advances and what Marlow comes up against is the incongruity of stern principles in the service of insupportable ends. His amazed observation of proficient organisation travestied by the accountant who keeps meticulous books in the midst of the trading station's 'inhabited devastation', his sardonic response to the Manager's cynical distinction between the company's random plunder and Kurtz's 'unsound methods', and his own insistence on 'the right way of going to work' in the employ of an outfit he knows to be bent on profit through pillage and of whose enterprises he had remarked with disgust, 'The work was going on. The work!' (p. 66), disclose Marlow's shock and show his beliefs to be untenable. He is the central protagonist and the principal mediator, but his credibility is not undisputed since his function as the ironic voice and disenchanted eye who disposes of imperialism's pretensions and reveals the disjunctions between its noble rhetoric and its squalid practice is undercut by the oblique commentary the fiction sustains on the alternative doctrines he advances, doctrines which measure his disaffection from official imperialism while articulating an impulse to discover positive qualities in a venture to which his society is dedicated; and it is by attaching moral purpose to imperialism that Marlow is cast as the innocent player who in speaking his lines announces his own errors of judgement.

The enemy of imperialism's conceited oratory, who uses its inflated vocabulary – the heavenly mission to civilise, humanise, improve and instruct, the noble cause of progress, the exalted trust, high and just proceedings, magnificent dependencies, emissaries of light – to revile the mendacity of its inventors and castigate its atrocious practice, is himself the author of a dissertation offering a conscience clause to a project he condemns as conscienceless:

> The conquest of the earth, which mostly means the taking it away from those who have a different complexion or slightly flatter noses than ourselves, is not a pretty thing when you look into it too much. What redeems it is the idea only. An idea at the back of it; not a sentimental pretence but an idea; and an unselfish belief in the idea – something you can set up, and bow down before, and offer a sacrifice to – (pp. 50–1)

Marlow returns to the words and images invoked to construct an imperialist ethos when he refers to the company agents in their station as 'resembling a lot of faithless pilgrims bewitched inside a rotten fence. The word "ivory" rang in the air, was whispered, was sighed. You would think they were praying for it' (p. 76), and again in describing the ceremonies where supine worshippers offered up 'unspeakable rites' to Kurtz. Yet while his narration is replete with sardonic insights, acerbic commentary and mordant wit, the ominous reverberations of transposing his indeterminate faith to situations where its impulse is obscenely parodied are spoken but not heard by Marlow.[10] The decisive subversion of his doctrine, with its disturbing affinities to the very rhetoric he despises and derides ['We want . . . for the guidance of the cause intrusted to us by Europe, so to speak, higher intelligence, wide

sympathies, a singleness of purpose' (p. 79)], is effected by the
dying Kurtz, his soul 'satiated with primitive emotions, avid of
lying fame, of sham distinction' (p. 147–8) when he raves about
the need for a successful colonialist to demonstrate commitment
to a judicious blend of material aims and pure ideals: 'You show
them you have in you something that is really profitable, and then
there will be no limits to the recognition of your ability . . . Of
course you must take care of the motives – right motives – always'
(p. 148).

It is then Marlow's own narration that negates his thesis on the
redemptive dimensions to imperialism. His confusions about the
substance of his narration, his misrecognitions, the discrepancies
between what he shows and what he sees, his positing of
certainties which prove to be dubious, these are the fiction's
means of exhibiting that his endeavour to devise an ethical basis
for imperialism is destined to fail. With the advent of Kurtz,
another narrative mode supervenes, submerging the existing
discourse in material that originates a new legend for colonial
mythology. Since the intercession of ironic disproof is here
suspended, the problem for the reader becomes one of distinguishing between what is spontaneously revealed and the formal
constructions brought to the evidence by Marlow's interpretative
commentary and, in the absence of a countermanding viewpoint,
implicitly endorsed by the fiction. From the information imparted
by Marlow, Kurtz emerges as exorbitant and grotesque because
of the excesses rather than the essence of his conduct, a figure
existing at the far end of the colonial continuum, the bizarre
features of which are noted by Marlow in language that is precise
and severe, registering his astonishment and outrage while
remaining coherent. He recalls watching a French man-of-war in
'the empty immensity of earth, sky and water . . . firing into a
continent', looking on the 'wanton smash-up' caused by the
Company's exploitation of physical and human resources, seeing
an emaciated, diseased and starving chain-gang 'in all the
attitudes of pain, abandonment and despair', and meeting agents
lacking in principle, imagination and intelligence who boasted
that 'Anything – anything can be done in this country' (p. 91). A
passage abundantly signposted with absurdities and atrocities
leads to Kurtz, the Company's most successful agent and one
reputed to have gone out to Africa with moral ideas of some sort.

It is with misgivings that the sceptical Marlow reads the Report commissioned from Kurtz by the International Society for the Suppression of Savage Customs, unwillingly electrified by its magniloquence and chilled by its final call to a holocaust: 'at the end of that moving appeal to every altruistic sentiment it blazed at you, luminous and terrifying, like a flash of lightning in a serene sky: "Exterminate all the brutes!" ' (p. 118). On meeting Kurtz, Marlow confronts a man impersonating imperialism's will to expand its domain over the earth and all its creatures, a spectacle for which his previous sights of a ravenous colonialism had prepared him: 'You should have heard him say, "My ivory." . . . "My intended, my ivory, my station, my river, my –" everything belonged to him' (p. 116); even his cannibalistic mien speaks of that insatiable appetite for conquest elevated to a principle by imperialism: 'I saw him open his mouth wide – it gave him a weirdly voracious aspect, as though he had wanted to swallow all the air, all the earth, all the men before him' (p. 134).[11]

All this is before Marlow and is the 'objective' substance of his graphically told story, but what he *sees*, and this remains uncontroverted by the text, belongs not to history but to fantasy, to the sensational world of promiscuity, idolatry, satanic rites and human sacrifices unveiled in nineteenth-century travellers' tales as the essence of an Africa without law or social restraint, a representation that was embroidered into colonial romances and charted by an ethnography still innocent of a discipline's necessary rules of evidence.[12] It is this mythological cosmos, an invention essential to imperialism's rationale, which fascinates Marlow and as the lurid images from colonialism's gallery take possession of his vision these, in the absence of a dissenting discourse, come to occupy the fiction's space. With this, there is a displacement of the perspective on Kurtz as a Prospero figure who had fled the society of his peers to enter a universe where the thunder and lightning of his technological magic had made him appear a god to the lakeside tribe of the wilderness; and the symbiotic relationship between Kurtz and his acolytes, which from Marlow's account had appeared as an extreme form of that sado-masochistic political nexus celebrated in colonial legend as a natural bond between a master-race and peoples born to servitude, is relegated to the margins of a vista now wholly filled by enactments of rituals that are native to Africa and violations of western taboos.[13]

What appals the much-travelled and worldly Marlow, who shows himself to be a convinced cultural-relativist since he is untroubled by 'uncomplicated savagery', able to accept cannibals as men one could work with, and not deeply disturbed at identifying the round knobs on the posts surrounding Kurtz's house as shrunken heads, is rumour of the rites initiated by Kurtz in his own honour. It is the atavistic regression of a cultivated European which alone elicits 'moral shock' in Marlow, 'as if something altogether monstrous, intolerable to thought and odious to the soul, has been thrust upon me unexpectedly' (p. 141). As Marlow struggles to explain Kurtz's defection from civilisation, so does his already opaque portrayal become hidden by a jungle of tropes:

> The wilderness had patted him on the head, and behold, it was like a ball – an ivory ball; it had caressed him, and lo! – he had withered; it had taken him, loved him, embraced him, got into his veins, consumed his flesh, and sealed his soul to its own by the inconceivable ceremonies of some devilish initiation . . . I think it had whispered to him things about himself which he did not know, things of which he had no conception till he took counsel with this great solitude – and the whisper had proved irresistibly fascinating . . . I tried to break the spell – the heavy, mute spell of the wilderness – that seemed to draw him to its pitiless breast by the awakening of forgotten and brutal instincts, by the memory of gratified and monstrous passions. (pp. 115, 131, 144)

Discernible through the thicket of the prose is the wilderness as a metonym for dangerous appetites curbed by civilisation, and Kurtz's liberation from repression, his 'forgetting himself' amongst the peoples of the tribe is seen as a capitulation to an enslavement in which he hates the life and is unable to get away. With this composite representation, Marlow's academic toler- ance of savagery is overwhelmed by articulations of a visceral revulsion towards the other that obliterate the fiction's existing definitions of that historical condition in which Kurtz's pursuit of profit and power had been nurtured and the specific circum- stances where the 'bounds of permitted aspiration' had appeared illimitable. Thus what finally commands attention is not the consummate exploiter poisoned by a diet too lavish and too rich, but the daemonic hero who had embraced outlawed experiences and who, because of gratifying illegitimate desires, was privileged to confirm the value of what he had profaned: 'Better his cry . . . It was an affirmation, a moral victory paid for by innumerable defeats, by abominable terrors, by abominable satisfactions. But it was a victory!' (p. 151).[14] The call to genocide uttered by the megalomaniac extremist who 'could get himself to believe anything', the rhetoric of the self-infatuated colonialist who having witnessed and committed atrocities had gone on to extol these as festivals of racial power, is finally drowned by the last whisper of the repentant iconoclast attaining heroic stature by acknowledging his sin in desecrating the commandments of his civilisation.

Marlow's mythopoeic narration of a journey in time to specified places in Africa's interior follows a route that had already been taken by the western mind through the alien world Europe set out to conquer, and if it arrives at the same destination, it selects other landmarks for scrutiny and locates the roots of western shock and antipathy in new areas. The fiction's inclusive view is derived from spanning both Marlow's conscious apprehensions and the information he unconsciously mediates; and it is by inventing meanings for Africa that he exhibits the geography and boundaries of the imperialist imagination, while also illuminating the dislocating effects of a foreign mode on a mind formed by the western experience and devoted to its forms.[15] His voyage along a formless, featureless coast, 'as if still in the making', past rapids whose rushing noise sounds 'as though the tearing pace of the launched earth had suddenly become audible', and into the virgin forest where the vegetation seems 'like a rioting invasion of soundless life . . . ready to topple over the creek, to sweep every little man of us out of his little existence' (p. 86), maps a mythic return of modern civilisation to an imagined primal condition and images a dream of the conscious mind regressing to its archaic ground: 'Going up that river was like travelling back to the earliest beginnings of the world . . . We were cut off from the comprehension of our surroundings . . . We could not understand because we were too far and could not remember, because we were travelling in the night of first ages, of those ages that are gone, leaving hardly a sign – and no memories' (pp. 92, 96).
From being a blank place on a map once seen by Marlow when

a boy dreaming of the adventures to come, Africa is experienced by the man who is now a servant of colonialism, as an alien cosmos whose every aspect violates his concepts of intelligibility and congruity. Its vacant landscape, without form or feature, is deaf, mute and petrified: 'An empty stream, a great silence, an impenetrable forest . . . It was not sleep – it seemed unnatural, like a state of trance. Not the faintest sound of any kind could be heard' (pp. 93, 101). In this proliferation of negatives, Marlow communicates a recoil from what he intuitively senses to be an immanent quietism annulling the rational orderings and moral discriminations imposed by western thought, and repudiating that affirmative activism to which as a sailor he is heir and which he considers the essential human attribute and appropriate field of endeavour:

> We penetrated deeper and deeper into the heart of darkness . . .
> We were wanderers on prehistoric earth, on an earth that wore the aspects of an unknown planet. We could have fancied ourselves the first of men taking possession of an accursed inheritance, to be subdued at the cost of profound anguish and excessive toil . . . The earth seemed unearthly. We are accustomed to look upon the shackled form of a conquered monster, but there – there you could look at a thing monstrous and free. (pp. 95, 96)

For Marlow Africa is the negation of his own humanly-dominated and dynamic social order, a domain where archaic energies are rampant and nature's exercise of an autonomous will is unlimited. However, competing with this perception which sets nature against culture as adversaries, is Marlow's insight that what is 'true' and 'real' is the human presence as modifier and modified within the material world, a relationship exhibited by Africans paddling a boat in the surf and violated by the careless greed of victors who savage what they have appropriated. In Kurtz, a man driven by a hunger to engorge the universe, the fiction displays the conqueror who despoils the planet he craves to possess, points to his fate as victim of its 'terrible vengeance for the fantastic invasion', and with this delivers a judgement on imperialism's awesome triumphalism:

> I had to deal with a being to whom I could not appeal in the name of anything high or low. I had, even like the niggers, to

invoke him – himself – his own exalted and terrible degradation. There was nothing either above or below him and I knew
it. He had kicked himself loose of the earth . . . he had kicked the
very earth to pieces. (p. 144)

Because the fiction does not dramatise a political struggle
between coloniser and colonised – indeed the human material for
such a treatment is absent as the blacks are not functional
protagonists but figures in a landscape who do not constitute a
human presence – the confrontation between Europe and Africa is
realised wholly as the conflict between two polarised and
incompatible epistemologies, an encounter which displays the
insufficiencies of positivism without endorsing metaphysics as an
alternative. The one disposition, articulated in ways austere and
ornamental by the primary narrators, Marlow and Kurtz,
represents the philosophy underpinning the project of an expansionist Europe mobilised to conquer and remake the earth;[16] the
other, silently manifest in Africa's primordial wilderness, intimates the existence of transcendental knowledge. For Marlow the
voyage through this other universe exposes the poverty of his own
outlook, and the man who is at home in the turbulence of the
temporal world, who abhors unreconstructed nature, is without a
religious sensibility and finds poetry in proficiency, is led to make
a distinction between the surface truths and accurate likenesses
accessible to empirical observation, which he contrasts favour-
ably with senseless delusion, splendid appearances and unreal
pretence, and the 'hidden truths' and 'overwhelming realities'
which can only be approached asymtotically and known
experientially. His journey comes to mimic an epistemological
passage taking him from faith in 'the unmistakably real', the
'redeeming . . . straight-forward facts of life', the world of rivets
and steamboats, mechanics and explicit navigational manuals
where chronology and duration prevail and work dignifies
existence, to intimations of other meanings manifest in a landscape he can only perceive metaphorically. The silent wilderness
strikes him 'as something great and invincible, like evil or truth';
'the silence of the land went home to one's very heart – its mystery,
its greatness, the amazing reality of its concealed life' (p. 80); the
woods seem to have an 'air of hidden knowledge' and in the
stillness of the jungle Marlow senses 'an implacable force
brooding over an inscrutable intention'.

The ornate and obscurantist language both intimates and conceals Marlow's intuition that there may be non-phenomenal 'realities' and alternative ways of perceiving 'truth', since this apprehension must contend with his commitment to pragmatism as necessary to efficiency: 'When you have to attend . . . to the mere incidents of the surface, the reality – the reality, I tell you, – fades. The inner truth is hidden – luckily, luckily' (p. 93). On the threshold of new ways of seeing, Marlow draws back from the dangers of too much reality to the boundaries of that restricted consciousness he had ventured to criticise. In turning away from the amorphous and indefinable absolutes perceived as indwelling in Africa, Marlow repudiates the wilderness to whose being he had responded with awe and humility, disparaging it as the habitation of those malignant energies his civilisation had defused: 'never, never before, did this land, this river, this jungle, the very arch of this blazing sky, appear to me so hopeless and so dark, so impenetrable to human thought, so pitiless to human weakness' (p. 127). His recoil from its 'tenebrous and passionate soul', 'the lurking death . . . the hidden evil . . . the profound darkness of its heart', 'the unseen presence of victorious corruption, the darkness of an impenetrable night', coalesces with the revulsion he feels for its indigenous peoples whose very presence in that desolation had amazed him. Together, the effluences from the spirit of the place and the sights of the human inhabitants giving corporeal form to that essence provide Marlow with an explanation of Kurtz's fall, an interpretation in which the fiction, for want of a dissenting viewpoint, concurs. Having crossed to the frontiers of the imperialist imagination and looked back on its narrow territory, Marlow retreats to its heartland taking the text with him and, in the range of his repugnance and opprobrium, initiating a new chapter in colonialist mythology.

For what the fiction validates is Marlow's conviction that the choice before a stranger exposed to an alien world lies between a rigorous adherence to ethnic identity, which carries the freight of remaining ignorant of the foreign,[17] or embracing the unknown and compromising racial integrity. His way, a posture that was traditionally enjoined by British imperialism on its servants, is opposed to Kurtz's dangerous intimacy with the other. However, both Kurtz and Marlow look upon blacks as another genus, the one psychotically hating those to whom he is tied by an illegitimate bond, the other reluctantly recognising a remote and distant kinship with people he sees ambivalently to be 'not inhuman' and whom he perceives either as noble savages aloof from the degradations of modern civilisation – the statuesque chain-gang walking slow and erect, the superb bearing of the barbarous woman, the profound, lustrous and enquiring look of the dying helmsman – or as a subspecies that has failed to realise its human potential.[18] If Marlow does formally acknowledge the unity of humankind and declares the human mind to be the repository of 'all the past as well as all the future', he also distances himself from the blacks, seeing their faces as grotesque masks, judging their souls to be rudimentary and their minds as belonging to the beginnings of time, and hearing their speech as a black and incomprehensible frenzy. It is finally by denying them the faculty of 'human' speech that Marlow delineates his cognition of the real and unbridgeable gulf, since apart from the laconic but eloquent announcement of Kurtz's death made by a servant in broken English, and the cannibal headman's curt request that hostile tribesmen be given to the crew for food, the blacks coming within his vista express themselves either in the 'violent babble of uncouth sounds' (p. 69) or through mime. It is language that draws Marlow towards Kurtz because he can speak English and it is Kurtz's voice that entices him into his orbit; on the other hand, it is his response to the 'terrible frankness' of the Africans' 'wild and passionate uproar' that for Marlow confirms verbal utterances as the primary form of consciousness and one in which the blacks do not partake: 'An appeal to me in this fiendish row – is there? Very well; I hear; I admit, but I have a voice, too, and for good or evil mine is the speech that cannot be silenced' (p. 97). This intrusion of testament into Marlow's narrative registers a powerful affirmation of faith in reason over instinct and passion, which in the context is a declaration of allegiance to Europe and an assertion of its stature.[19] That is why Marlow, who had accepted the cannibal helmsman as a partner and acknowledged the 'claims of distant kinship' in his dying look, can sacrifice this obligation to the greater loyalty owing a man who has disobeyed every tenet of his creed but to whom he is bound through the umbilical cord of culture, and in this he demonstrates an act of solidarity with a world whose values he suspects and whose practices he disavows.

The scornful voices in *Heart of Darkness* castigating the 'dead cats

of civilisation' and the 'dust-bins of progress' echo the fears
expressed by Conrad's contemporaries, optimistic socialists and
authoritarian pessimists alike, that the West was embarking on a
course that would lead to its own destruction. In the fiction's
universe, Europe does not manifest itself as the vital force of
progress proposed by imperialist propaganda, but as the parent of
degenerate progeny, of sordid ambitions pursued by corrupt
human agents. Yet, having detached readers from spontaneous
trust in imperialism's rationale, the fiction introduces themes
valorising the doctrine of cultural allegiance as a moral imperative which is independent of the community's collective moral
conduct. It is to this end that the adumbrations of racist views, the
denigration of a foreign structure of experience and the commendation of submission to civilisation's discontents are directed,
strategies that clear the way for sanctioning Marlow's lie in
defence of Europe. Since the historical and mythopoeic modes
intersect and diverge, the fiction can register ethical stances as
disconnected from social circumstances, so that Marlow's negoti-
ation of his dilemma is not acknowledged as constituting a
political choice. Attention is instead focused on Marlow as the
dissident hero who stands by the dying renegade and solaces his
spellbound betrothed, and the principled traitor whose honourable behaviour entails a violation of his own creed. On every score
but one, Marlow can be seen to be placed in situations where his
austere standards are compromised and his beliefs sacrificed; to
the code of gallantry alone does he remain defiantly faithful and
the recipients of his chivalry are the contrary and complementary
incarnations of a Europe formally committed to humanism and
humanitarianism while negating these in the pursuit of imperialist ambitions.

   That Marlow admits to an inconsequential lie and makes this
the occasion for a peroration on the malignancy of falsehood,
while failing to recognise the import of the real lie when he
protects Kurtz's reputation in Europe with evasions and by
deliberate deception abets the exalted fantasies of the Intended, is
the fiction's means of showing up Marlow's capacity for self-
delusion and the strength of a commitment to Europeanism which
blinds him to the act as one that is a betrayal of his principles. If
Kurtz, musician and poet, orator and artist, writer and colonial
agent, to whose making 'All Europe contributed', is the embodiment of the West's secular culture and the incarnation of its

expansionist impulse, then the Intended with her fair hair, pale visage and pure brow, her mature capacity for fidelity, belief and suffering, is the emblem of Europe's religious traditions and the symbol of an imperialism saved by visionary desires. Of his faithfulness to Kurtz, Marlow speaks as if this had been pre-destined, 'it was ordered I should never betray him – it was written I should be loyal to the nightmare of my choice' (p. 141), and he does not apply to himself the stern judgement he had made on the intrepid Russian sailor's dangerous and fatalistically accepted devotion to Kurtz. Marlow, however, had resisted the seduction of Kurtz's magnetic presence and offered his support to one who despite transgressions was a sentient product of the western world. Drawn to the Intended by 'an impulse of unconscious loyalty', Marlow defers to this figure of a virtuous Europe in full knowledge that the object of his homage is a fantasy representation of a real social order. In delivering to her the lie about her beloved and colonialism's civilising mission, carried out as she believes by great and good men of generous minds and noble hearts, Marlow is fulfilling a romantic obligation to protect bourgeois ladies like the Intended and his aunt, who also confidently mouths imperialist cant, within 'that beautiful world of their own, lest ours get worse', a world which if set up 'would go to pieces before the first sunset' (p. 59).

While this suggests the gallant defence of idealism against pragmatism, Marlow's motivation, like the notion of chivalry itself, is tainted with suspect attitudes since he evokes two contrasting but related images of women to serve respectively as figures of Europe's casuistry and its delusions. Just as Kurtz's sketch of a blindfolded woman carrying a lighted torch which has a sinister effect on her face represents an unseeing Europe confidently holding a beacon on to it knows not what in Africa, so does the Intended, whose features bear the delicate shade of truthfulness, and who demands confirmation of her mistaken beliefs, stand as the false prophetess of imperialism's utopian impulse. All the same it is 'before the faith that was in her, before that great and saving illusion that shone with an unearthly glow in the darkness' (p. 159), that Marlow bows his head, a reverent gesture evoking his earlier exhortation of fealty to an unselfish belief in an idea, 'something you can set up, and bow down before, and offer a sacrifice to –'. But now because the eulogies to blind devotion are not undercut by the ironies attaching to its enactment by the vile agents worshipping ivory or the adorers crawling before Kurtz, the fiction invites a positive response to Marlow's action which its cumulative discussion has counter-manded.

Marlow assents to the fallacies of an ignorant woman, but confesses to his knowing companions, men themselves connected with colonial ventures and therefore fellow-conspirators whose absolution from the lie he seeks and whose complicity in the lie he solicits and will receive, since on that silence about imperialism's practice depends the utterance of its high-minded and menda-cious justifications. The address of the primary narrator to a contemporary British audience began with the appearance of flattering their self-esteem as a nation of intrepid and virtuous empire-builders, and ended by disturbing their conscience and undermining their confidence. Marlow on the other hand makes known at the outset his contempt for imperialism's sententious verbiage, and although his narration abundantly validates his view of colonialism as robbery with violence, his story concludes with an affirmation of loyalty to Europe's illusory pure form. Since Marlow is an unreliable witness and his tale the unburden-ing of a nonconformist moralist who has by his own standards compromised his individual integrity in the name of a higher corporate obligation, neither his admonition nor his approbation carry the seal of textual approval, and the contradictions in his stance are made transparent through the ironic juxtapositions of the 'facts' he is narrating and his own interpretation of these situations. That Marlow the adherent of an austere code of serious service and Kurtz the flamboyant practitioner of the triumphalist aspiration are products of the same social order and servants of the same official social ends, is an unacceptable reality that Marlow is unable to assimilate and that the text itself intimates but does not confront. The fact of the book's existence does give credence to the argument that *Heart of Darkness* is ultimately a public disavowal of imperialism's authorised lies. But although the central dialogue is conducted by Marlow's two voices speaking in counterpoint, one the sardonic and angry dissident denouncing imperialism's means and goals as symptoms of the West's moral decline, the other the devoted member of this world striving to recover a utopian dimension to its apocalyptic ambitions, the fiction's relationship to its principal intelligence is equivocal, giving and withholding authority to his testimony, exposing and occluding his inconsistencies. The joining of disparities in unorthodox and unexpected conjunctions is a deliberate and ostentatious feature of the novel's discourse, and the phrases 'abominable satisfactions', 'exalted degradation' and 'diabolic love' are overt signs of its heterogenous and incompatible meanings. These discontinuities have evoked conflicting readings and to proffer an interpretation of *Heart of Darkness* as a militant denunciation and a reluctant affirmation of imperialist civilisation, as a fiction that exposes and colludes in imperialism's mystifications, is to recognise its immanent contradictions.

3 *The Rescue: A Romance of the Shallows*

The consensus that *The Rescue* is a negligible work, interesting because of the prolonged difficulties Conrad had with its writing rather than because of any intrinsic properties, has overlooked its originality in telling a sumptuous tale of colonial adventure as a bleak political allegory divesting colonialism's heroic age of its eminent reputation.[1] In the body of Conrad's fictional engagements with the imperialist experience, this work is conspicuous for honouring and refuting colonialist myth, since the narrative discourse laments the ignominious failure of those noble impulses it set out to celebrate, the figurations animate the forms of the colonial imagination and display these as a mode of perception which signally fails to see, and the action, which dramatises the confrontation of the 'primitive' East with the 'sophisticated' West, supersedes its own conventional terms of reference to contemplate the conflict as one between two authentic universes ordered on dissimilar principles and adhering to different systems of value.[2] Initially conceived as the retrospective foundation of *Almayer's Folly* (1895) and *An Outcast of the Islands* (1896) to comprise an informal trilogy written in reverse chronological order, *The Rescue* in working out its themes breaks with the predominant outlook of the companion pieces and it is these divergent tendencies, incipient in the manuscript text and major discontinuities in the final form, that are the source of the fiction's stature as the work of an enlarged and disenchanted historical imagination, reviewing representations of an era that had already been constituted as history.

Between 1896 and 1899 Conrad worked intermittently and with perpetual frustration on the first version, 'The Rescuer',[3] unsuccessfully returning to it in 1916 and at last completing the work in 1918–19 by revising the existing text and producing new material for the as yet unwritten latter section.[4] Because the

40

finished novel is the product of different periods in the writer's life, it inevitably contains Conrad's *pentimento*; original intentions and first thoughts are visible in the revisions,[5] adding technical inconsistencies to the text's organic contradictions, but when read alongside the manuscript version, giving access to the ways in which Conrad reordered previously intractable material, altera- tions which abundantly justify his retrospective remarks that in the original he had been unable to transform his intentions into an appropriate fictional form.[6] If the exclusion of luminous passages[7] is a loss to a finished work which perversely retains ornate and merely decorative description, flaccid interpositions and man- nered dialogue, as well as coy and condescending comments on Malayan life and customs which can persuade readers that this is indeed a colonial romance, then the excision of ostentatious and sententious writing makes space for the expansion of the fiction's austere preoccupations. By defamiliarising the received assump- tions of the genre, Conrad transformed a melodramatic scenario about a catastrophe in the life of a colonial adventurer, set in picturesque surroundings and enacted in the midst of a mysteri- ous atmosphere, into a tragedy where the warring impulses, divided loyalties and ultimate defection of a protagonist who is both betrayer and betrayed, signify that larger crisis endemic to the European presence in the other hemisphere.

In finally calling the work *The Rescue: A Romance of the Shallows*,[8] Conrad declares an ironic engagement with its themes, an approach which defies the conventions of the colonial novel and reverses expectations of a romantic adventure tale triumphantly consummated. For the cost of releasing the European travellers captured by a local chieftain when their yacht is grounded in the shallow waters of the islands, is the death of Hassim and Immada, the exiled Malayan chieftains who had saved and been saved by Lingard, and whose usurped kingdom he is pledged to restore, and with their deaths the loss of 'his own soul'. The sardonic ambiguity of the title is repeated in naming the fiction's parts: if 'The Man and his Brig' promises the illustrious story of a buccaneer in command of his fate, then it delivers a fable about a fallible person of infinite illusions who relinquishes his autonomy and sacrifices his 'devotion to the greatness of an idea' for the transports of sexual passion. 'The Shore of Refuge', where the exiles have found shelter with the Arab ruler Balarab, is the place in which Lingard abandons his 'fierceness of purpose', deserting those who have given their future into his care, while 'The Capture', literally referring to the seizing of the yacht, alludes to the hold that Mrs Travers gains over Lingard, an infatuation which impairs rational thinking, paralyses will and immerses him in sublime indifference. Lingard experiences this enslavement as 'The Gift of the Shallows', a location which is also 'the shelter of his dreams . . . his hopes'; conversely it intimates the surrender of his independence to a woman of dubious probity and a retreat into a state where 'Every thought of action had become odious' (p. 246). The last subtitles announcing the contests dramatised by the fiction are, however, without sceptical resonances: 'The Point of Honour and the Point of Passion' testifies to Lingard's struggle with opposing feelings, the irreconcilable demands made on his resources and the competing calls on his allegiance, while 'The Claim of Life and the Toll of Death' witnesses the fatal outcome of his acts and neglects.

Yet while the action animates the moral dilemmas confronting the European inserted into the fissured colonial situation, the narrative discourse, through allocating privileged viewpoints to protagonists who are blind to the nature of colonialism, deflects attention away from the fiction's intrinsically political vision. In a novel narrated by an impersonal voice and where discrepancies of viewpoint inhere in the disjunctions between what the story demonstrates and how this is interpreted, a quasi-choral function is assigned to a peripheral character and a marginal man, who with his 'natural gift of insight' watches, speculates and prophesies. It is D'Alcacer who discerns Lingard's qualities and flaws, dubs him the Man of Fate and foresees his tragic destiny; it is his sceptical view of Edith Travers, whom he suspects of wanting in good faith, sincerity and honour, that despoils Lingard's image of her truth, courage and wisdom; it is he who detects the enduring accord underlying the evident incompatibility between the unconventional lady and her conformist husband, and it is his cynical recognition of the common ground which he, a Spanish nobleman, shares with the English bourgeoisie, that establishes the unity of the northern peoples and underlines their spontaneous alienation from foreign worlds. For while keenly aware of the nuances in the deportment of the whites, the Malayans are to him incomprehensible beings, 'gorgeous barbarians' whose existence he can only perceive as a deviation from western norms. Here D'Alcacer mediates one of the fiction's perspectives on the confrontation between the 'primitive' and the 'sophisticated', for whereas the variations in the class origins of the Europeans and the gradations in their responses to confinement amidst outlandish surroundings are discriminating observations of social conduct, the islanders are archetypal figures, noble in their bearing, poetic in their speech and romantic in their dress, who perform set-pieces and strike attitudes expressive of a narrow range of extreme emotions.

The effect of such a representation is that the Malayan protagonists are denied equal weight with the Europeans on the scales of Lingard's conflict, a deliberate imbalance formalised by the outlook of D'Alcacer who is unaware of the dimensions of Lingard's predicament and encourages Mrs Travers in her decision to withhold from him the urgent message recalling him to his promise. If D'Alcacer in his oblique yet authoritative mediations offers a vista which excludes the heart of the fiction's matter, then the foregrounding of Lingard's doomed affair with Mrs Travers, in which the nature of his passion and her response are communicated through purple writing and misty evasions, completes the process of diverting attention from the inscribed political perspective, since Lingard's choice of loyalty between the Europeans and the Malayans is made insignificant by the enormity of his obsession. As chance and accident, misunderstanding and confusion conspire in producing the final disaster, Lingard emerges not as the autonomous figure initially projected who by his deeds and omissions precipitates a cataclysm, but as the helpless victim of malign circumstances. In retreating to the conventions of the colonial novel, a fiction that has the potential to interrogate the ethos of colonialism by disappointing the anticipations so abundantly satisfied in popular literature eclipses its imminent critique of colonialism.

The Rescue harks back to times when colonialism was still innocent of the concerted thrust later organised by international finance capitalism, and the narrative discussion parodies the official rhetoric of this earlier era, innovates another commemorating the visionary aspirations of its pioneers, and shows both to be imaginary representations of the circumstances and relationships they profess to conceptualise. The inert and implacable clichés of colonialist propaganda about the duty to civilise and the necessary sacrifice of inferior races in the cause of orderly progress are spoken by the obtuse Mr Travers, who although a financier and politician active in furthering the expansion of the British Empire, is without the cosmic ambitions ritually enacted by a Kurtz and historically pursued by a Holroyd. As mouthed by Travers, such arguments, lacking the grandiloquence of fanaticism or the sagaciousness of casuistry, expose themselves as patently cosmetic and invite instant dismissal. Instead, what commands attention is the eloquent case made by the impersonal narrative voice for the independent and intrepid buccaneers of colonialism's halcyon age:

> Almost in our own day we have seen one of them – a true adventurer in his devotion to his impulse – a man of high mind and of pure heart, lay the foundations of a flourishing state on the ideas of pity and justice. He recognised chivalrously the claims of the conquered; he was a disinterested adventurer, and the reward of his noble instincts is in the veneration with which a strange and faithful race cherish his memory.
>
> Misunderstood and traduced in life, the glory of his achievement has vindicated the purity of his motives. He belongs to history. But there were others – obscure adventurers who had not his advantages of birth, position and intelligence; who had only his sympathy with the people of the forests and sea he understood and loved so well. (pp. 3–4)

This speech exists intact in the manuscript but because the ironies attending the panegyric do not inhere in the speaker's mode of address, which contains no counterpoint and is without equivocations, its reverberations only become audible in the final version where the progress of Lingard's fall is witnessed. Since the passage is placed at the start of the finished novel, it has the status of a thesis whose axioms are to be spectacularly invalidated by the fiction's action, for *The Rescue* is the biography of one such obscure adventurer who is formally introduced as the incarnation of those very qualities eulogised by the narrator and who by his deeds refutes the legend. In Lingard, the lone and uprooted Englishman who pits his courage and ingenuity against Dutch power for a share in the spoils of the Malayan archipelago, the fiction offers a plebian counterpart to the aristocratic Rajah Brooke, a historical figure much admired by Conrad.[9] Lingard is himself presented as the stuff of future myth, a worthy comrade of audacious men long dead who, were they to haunt the places where they had once toiled, 'might have seen a white long-boat, pulled by eight oars and steered by a man sunburnt and bearded, a cabbage-leaf hat on his head, and pistols in his belt, skirting the black mud, full of twisted roots, in search of a likely opening' (p. 94).[10] With Lingard's apostasy, the affirmations of the idiosyncratic colonial creed advanced by the fiction[11] are undercut, the mystique of the chivalrous and disinterested adventurer is stripped away, leaving the more ambiguous figure of a maverick and dreamer motivated by altruism and self-interest, compassion and egoism, a man cut off from his ethnic roots and without roots in his place of exile, who aspires to create a new human collectivity under his rule and succeeds in disrupting an existing community.

What the fiction shows is Lingard's insoluble predicament in having to choose between fidelity to a heterodox commitment freely given to his Malayan clients, and his socially ordained obligations to persons of his own race who are also his class enemies; faced with such incompatible allegiances Lingard, as if in obedience to fate, comes to serve his masters and abandon his dependants. The 'protecting affection' he had extended to Hassim, Immada and their followers proves a faithless embrace, an outcome cynically anticipated by a chieftain musing on Lingard's determination to safeguard the yacht people at any price: 'After all, it was perhaps a great folly to trust any white man, no matter how much he seemed estranged from his own people' (p. 296). The Lingard of *The Rescue* is distinguished from his former incarnations in the preceding novels of the trilogy in that he is given a specific social history spanning an obviously circumscribed and disaffected working-class past, and an apparently unconfined and fulfilled colonial present. The child of Devon fishermen, Lingard progresses from collier-youth, trawler-boy and gold-digger to become owner of a brig in the archipelago, but having wandered 'beyond that circle which race, early associations, all the essential conditions of one's origin, trace around every man's life' (pp. 121–2), the trader now esteemed throughout the islands remembers that he is one of England's dispossessed, and when the yacht people happen upon his cosmos, he looks on them as creatures from another planet, 'unattainable, infinitely remote'.[12]

The powerfully built and passionate freebooter thus faces the dapper and formal Travers, capitalist and man of affairs, as a

life-long enemy, disdainfully reminding his adversary, who scorns
him as an adventurer, that the alternative open to him would have
been 'to starve or work at home for such people as you' (p. 134).
From D'Alcacer whom he recognises as one of 'their kind',
Lingard keeps his distance; however the poised and handsome
Mrs Travers neutralises his implacable hostility to the rich and
the powerful, which gives way to an erotic servitude feeding on his
humble birth and her high rank.[13] Thus when she demands of him
that he save the lives of her companions, he imagines himself as a
mythic hero fighting wars for love, even entertaining a fantasy of
decimating the Settlement which is the homeland of his allies and
the refuge of the exiles. Concurrent with this bewitchment and
inseparable from it, is Lingard's capitulation to the interests of the
white travellers, each step in the process loosening his ties with
Hassim and Immada, even as he continues to insist to Mrs
Travers that the bonds are indissoluble: 'What are you to me
against these two? If I were to die here on the spot would you care?
No one would care at home. No one in the whole world – but these
two' (p. 158). When Mrs Travers, repelled and alarmed at the
hold the Malayans have over Lingard, makes a calculated effort to
conjure up the heritage and memories they share, his response is
to affirm the chasm between them by stating that his recollections
are of 'Poverty, hard work – and death . . . And now I've told you,
and you don't know. That's how it is between us. You talk to me –
I talk to you – and we don't know' (pp. 218–19).

    The transition from confronting the yacht people as a free man,
to becoming their servant, a direction imperceptible to Lingard
but followed with despair by his allies and dependants, is
measured by his changing use of 'my people'. Initially outraged at
Hassim's reference to the whites as 'your people', Lingard
denounces this usage to Mrs Travers: 'My people! Are you? How
much? Say – how much? You're no more mine than I am yours.
Would any of you fine folks at home face black ruin to save a
fishing smack's crew from getting drowned?' (pp. 164–5). But
with the transfer of his primary allegiance, he comes to name them
as 'my own people', reminding Hassim of his promise to be 'A
friend to all whites who are of my people, forever' (p. 234),[14]
thereby delineating his fundamental loyalty and denying those
whom his aide Jörgenson knows to be 'his people'. As Lingard
becomes wholly preoccupied with securing the release of the
Europeans and obsessed with remaining near Mrs Travers, a

need which increasingly leads to prevarication and indecision, he 'forgets' Hassim and Immada, finding them unreal, wounded at their gentle reprimands, shamed by their devotion.[15] Even before the final abandonment, Lingard had already symbolically disavowed his former friends by giving to Mrs Travers the costly garments intended for Immada, a dispossession recognised by the recipient who sees that she is robbing the girl of more than her clothes. Angered at Lingard's vacillations, Mrs Travers challenges him to choose between 'these much-tried people' and the Europeans, deliberately recalling him from a commitment for which she had earlier expressed admiration, and urging him to accept responsibility for his compatriots who are innocent bystanders in a jungle dispute.[16] With the growth of his obsession with her, Lingard's defection is complete; having fled subservience to the ruling class in England, he now submits to them in the East, a situation whose ironies are observed by Hassim's follower Jaffir when he reminds him that his greatness derives from his position in the islands and asks, 'But what becomes of the strength of your arms before your own white people? Where does it go to, I say? (p. 334).

Amidst an alien landscape the Europeans enact their metropolitan class enmities and manifest their racial solidarity, and the highly theatrical encounter between the worldly and mature Mrs Travers and the innocent Immada makes plain Lingard's choice between irreconcilable obligations when the two women compete for Lingard's love and loyalty, the one exploiting his infatuation with her to compel him to acknowledge the priority of the Europeans' interest, the other urging him to stay faithful to his pledge: 'Do not look at that woman . . . look away – look at us . . . You are a cruel woman! You are driving him away from where his strength is. You put madness into his heart!' (pp. 218, 234).[17] This melodramatic encounter displays the callousness of a heroine and the weakness of a hero in a scenario where a conviction of cultural superiority authorises the one and ethnic fealty determines the other. But with the catastrophe he has brought about, Lingard turns his back on the yacht people, liberating himself once more from class subservience, and by refusing the excuse of an 'accident' and accepting expulsion from his paradisiacal island retreat, acknowledges the consequences of his betrayal. 'Belarab, standing in front of a group of headmen, pretended not to see the white people as they went by. With Lingard he shook hands,

murmuring the usual formulas of friendship; and when he heard
the great white man say, "You shall never see me again," he felt
immensely relieved' (p. 443). The circle is complete: as the
adventurer who was once seen discovering an entrance to the
secret Shore of Refuge leaves the island, the people of dark creek
and impenetrable forest resume an existence disturbed but not yet
destroyed by the western invasion.

In telling the story of Lingard's doomed enterprise, *The Rescue*
raises new questions about authorised colonial postures. 'The
Rescuer' had Wyndham, a successful gentleman-adventurer,
warn Lingard of the dire consequences of intimacy with the local
people:

> Don't go in too deep with them . . . I say to you *don't*. Take a
> warning from me; I can't get away now . . . I am ready to go –
> but I can't. I've given myself up to them. Never do that – never.
> Be loyal, be honest with them – but don't allow yourself to like
> anyone. You will regret it – too late. We are no better, perhaps,
> but we are different. There is about them a fascination . . . the
> fascination of primitive ideas – of primitive virtues perhaps.
> Something enticing and bitter in the life – in the thought around
> you, if you once step into the world of their notions. Very bitter.
> We can never forget our origin. Like no one. Don't give yourself
> up. Primitive virtues are poison to us – white men. We have
> gone on different lines. Look on, trade, make money . . . Above
> all don't fight with them. That's how it begins. First you fight
> with them – then you fight for them – no closer tie than spilt
> blood – then you begin to think they are human beings . . . They
> are – very. That's the worst of it – for when you begin to see it
> your ideas change. You . . . see injustice and cruel folly of what,
> before, appeared just and wise. Then you begin to love them –
> that fascination you know. ('The Rescuer', pp. 140–2)

These admonitions, which have affinities to Marlow's meditations on relationships between the races, conform in the spirit, if
not the wording, to the orthodox imperialist prohibition against
the invaders assimilating to the native culture because this meant
moral weakness and led inevitably to moral degradation. Wyndham and his homilies are, however, absent from *The Rescue*, as
they must be since the substance of his dogma is irrelevant to the

fiction's action, and although the vocabulary alluding to the threat of the other is retained, what is developed is the connection between ethnic exclusiveness and the colonialist posture, or obversely, the dispositions leading the white person to abdicate from the imperialist role.

Indeed the fiction inverts the assumptions informing the 'conquest/surrender' dichotomy that Conrad posed in contemplating the stranger's encounter with a foreign world. Because Jörgenson, who had 'gone native' retains an unwavering fidelity to his commitments, while Lingard who dominates his environment and asserts his authority as a white man is unfaithful to a trust, what is demonstrated is that 'surrender' can imply and reinforce integrity, whereas the stance of the conqueror can vitiate moral fibre. In the story of Lingard's renegacy the fiction explores the nature and limits of colonial paternalism, disclosing flaws in the posture of white men who, through the advantages of their civilisation's technology, became kings in the other hemisphere. Without honour in his own land, Lingard had exiled himself to a distant archipelago, there commanding the titles of Rajah Laut, Ruler of the Seas, and King Tom, and establishing a relationship with his Malayan crew and the island people, resting on their deference, feeding his hunger for mastery and disabling their autonomy.[18] When as a 'romantic necessity' Lingard had impulsively pledged himself to the cause of Hassim and Immada, it was out of a sense of obligation aroused by their passivity and dumb quietude: 'what appealed to him most was the silent, the complete, unquestioning, and apparently incurious, trust of these people' (p. 88).[19] From a position of unchallenged authority, Lingard can ignore the warnings of Jörgenson, himself once an adventurer and victim of a failed coup he had engineered, against meddling in the political affairs of the islands, since his involvement is not a submission to the will of the people but a further exercise of his racial power. In his dealings with the Malayans, Lingard, whose brig is the visible sign of his might within their land, had always reminded them of his power: 'I am Rajah here. This bit of country is all my own' (p. 75), and his defiant statement to Travers, 'I am where I belong. And I belong where I am' (p. 121), is not a declaration of assimilation but of the special status he had won. Lingard had come to know the sea changes and coast's contours as intimately as the Malayan seamen who navigated without mechanical aids, and in a culture where 'time is nothing' and 'life and activities are not ruled by the clock' (p. 415), his brig with its gunwale, muskets, sailing instruments and time pieces represents an invading force, while the man himself is proof against the seductions of a mesmeric landscape, exerting his will to resist the hallucinatory effect of a still and silent land offering peace.

Lingard acknowledges his affinities with Jörgenson but it is the distinctions between the motives and actions of the two men that define two distinctive stances and in so doing reverse the value judgement attaching to 'conquest' and 'surrender'. For it is this 'slave at a feast', this 'skeleton at the gaming table', this phantom, shade, haunting spirit, wreck, ghostly and indifferent corpse, who is the fiction's unacknowledged hero, a man of firm principle, moved by injustice, loyal to his aged Malayan girl, a traitor to imperialism's cause, revered by the island people for whom Belarab speaks when he recalls how he had joined them in their struggle against the Dutch colonisers: 'And there was amongst us . . . one white man who remained to the end, who was faithful with his strength, with his courage, and with his wisdom. A great man. He had great riches, but a greater heart' (pp. 111–12). Entrusted by Lingard to oversee the plans of the invasion that will restore Hassim and Immada to their kingdom, Jörgenson acts with competence and dedication. His decision to send Jaffir as emissary to warn Lingard of dissension and vacillation amongst his allies is prompted by 'the simple wish to guide Lingard's thoughts in the direction of Hassim and Immada, to help him to make up his mind at last to a ruthless fidelity to his purpose' (p. 384). In Jörgenson's code, they and not the Europeans are Lingard's 'own people', and he regards it as just that Lingard's fate should be as his was, 'to be absorbed, captured, made their own either in failure or in success . . . What he really wanted Lingard to do was to cease to take the slightest interest in those whites – who were the sort of people that left no footprints' (p. 388). When Lingard fails to respond to his communications, Jörgenson takes this as a desertion and blows up the boat from which the invasion was to have been launched, an act which Lingard later understands: 'he gave me my chance – before he gave me up' (p. 465).

Jörgenson thus survives the denigratory narrative commentary that accompanies his every appearance and is calculated to draw attention to his evident failure, his defeated and demoralised condition, his indifference to the world of men, his inhabiting a realm of eternal oblivion. Nor do his lamentations at having given himself up to people, 'who have a devil of their own' with the loss of his youth, wealth and strength, impair the image of his steadfastness and incorruptible honour. What stands out is not the reprobate white man sunk in the mire of native life, but an heroic figure who comprehends every thought and purpose of the island people 'as if they were his own', and who is therefore free from the pressures to submit to white solidarity. For him 'The existence of those whites had no meaning on earth. They were the sort of people that pass without leaving footprints' (p. 384), a statement testifying to a severance of all bonds connecting him to the world of colonial power. Whereas Mrs Travers and Immada come together as strangers and part as enemies, the relationship between Jörgenson and Jaffir anticipates a possibility, rigorously denied by a discourse registering the disparities between West and East and negated by a symbolism signifying antinomy and antagonism, of a meeting place beyond the world made by imperialism: 'Twilight enveloped the two figures forward while they talked, looking in the stillness of their pose like carved figures of European and Asiatic contrasted in intimate contact' (pp. 378–9). Having formally introduced Lingard as the disinterested adventurer enacting the life of colonialist chivalry in his relationships with the colonial people, altruistically devoted to those he had made his dependants and who had made him rich and powerful, the fiction covertly and against its own grain displays the outcast Jörgenson, who has rejected the colonialist role, as the true knight-errant who will be cherished in the memory of a strange and faithful race, while Lingard is banished from the land and joins the ranks of those who leave no footprints: 'Lingard walked to the beach by himself, feeling a stranger to all men and abandoned by the All-Knowing God' (p. 444).

Although the narrative commentary alludes to the struggles of the island peoples against the Dutch, Portuguese, Spanish and English who had robbed them of their land and incited internecine strife, it is not an historical conflict that is dramatised but the spiritual schism within a world formally joined by imperialism. This discord is animated in the encounters between Immada and Mrs Travers, embodiments of the primitive and the sophisticated, intuition and reason, the Id and the Ego. The first meeting between the two women is seen by D'Alcacer as the coming together of discrepant and unequal realms, of epochs separated by aeons which momentarily touch and necessarily part: 'Mrs Travers fixed her eyes on Immada. Fair-haired and white she asserted herself before the girl of olive face and raven locks with the maturity of perfection, with the superiority of the flower over the leaf, of the phrase that contains a thought over the cry that can only express an emotion. Immense spaces and countless ages stretched between them' (p. 140). D'Alcacer's subsequent recollections centre on the symbolic disparity their presence registers, 'the beginning and the end, the flower and the leaf, the phrase and the cry' (p. 148), a dissimilarity made visible by the brilliant whiteness of the one and the luminous darkness of the other. To the infatuated Lingard Mrs Travers seems to shed an inspirational light leading him on to perform heroic deeds, to the admiring but cool D'Alcacer, who had known her in England, her lustre seems the artificial product of a splendid urban milieu, while to Immada, who is repelled by her appearance, her brightness is menacing: 'Have you seen her eyes shining under her eyebrows like rays of light darting under the arched boughs in a forest? They pierced me' (p. 242). Because light in the fiction is invariably lurid, glaring, awful and ghastly, without kindly or illuminating qualities, the suspect nature of Mrs Travers's dazzling complexion, white throat and pale hair is confirmed, and when placed near the dark warmth of the girl who turns on her 'eyes black as coal, sparkling and soft like a tropical night' (p. 141), Mrs Travers's radiance shows up as factitious: 'There were no shadows on her face; it was fiercely lighted, hermetically closed, of impenetrable fairness' (p. 214).

The sensuous pleasures evoked by the similes attached to black and the uncongenial connotations associated with white serve to invite sympathy for the qualities of the colonial world, and if this is precariously maintained and soon abandoned, it is superseded by the impulse to comprehend the immanent meanings of a culture pursuing ends remote from western concepts of value. The imagery of a land that is quiescent, somnolent and silent, an 'unconscious dream world', transfigures a physical location into a state of Nirvana, free of tension, want or desire: 'A great stillness had laid its hand over the earth, the sky, and the men; upon the immobility of landscape and people . . . Everything was still, empty, incandescent and fantastic' (pp. 114, 288). Significantly, all the settings, from the Shore of Refuge to the distant Wajo country, are shown as existing in a state of profound repose, and if the noisy, boisterous centres of trade, politics and agriculture peopled by skilled seamen, intrepid warriors, wily rulers and energetic cultivators do exist on the fringes of the fiction's quotidian world, they form no essential part of its ideological prospect. In abandoning the opening passages of 'The Rescuer' and removing the exotic tropes and approbrious analogues of the original, Conrad in the final version achieved a starker and more precisely focused representation of the quietest condition. Gone are the images of pullulating corruption, decay and death;[20] instead the coast is a petrified figure of nullity whose featureless geography defies western concepts of form, congruity, meaning and value and signifies a regression to the apparent stasis of inorganic life:

> The calm was absolute, a dead, flat calm, the stillness of a dead sea and of a dead atmosphere. As far as the eye could reach there was nothing but an impressive immobility. Nothing moved on earth, on the waters, and above them in the unbroken lustre of the sky . . . The coast off which the little brig, floating upright above her anchor, seemed to guard the high hull of the yacht has no distinctive features. It is land without form. It stretches away without cape or bluff, long and low – indefinitely; and when the heavy gusts of the northeast monsoon drive the thick rain slanting over the sea, it is seen faintly under the grey sky, black and with a blurred outline like the straight edge of a dissolving shore. In the long season of unclouded days, it presents to view only a narrow band of earth that appears crushed flat upon the vast level of waters by the weight of the sky, whose immense dome rests on it in a line as fine and true as that of the sea horizon itself . . .

> There was not a star in the sky and no gleam on the water; there was no horizon, no outline, no shape for the eye to rest upon, nothing for the hand to grasp. An obscurity that seemed without limit in space and time had submerged the universe like a destroying flood . . .

> All colour seemed to have gone out of the world. The oncoming shadow rose as subtle as a perfume from the black coast lying athwart the eastern semicircle; and such was the silence within

the horizon that one might have fancied oneself come to the end
of time. (pp. 5, 63, 241, 425)[21]

Such writing, with its plethora of negatives, its images of nullity,
and its perceptions of mythic time which is indifferent to duration,
brings to mind Forster's later and better known transfigurations
of the quiescence immanent in the formless, eternal and infinite
landscape of the Marabars.[22]

But if the affinities of phrase, image and cadence are evident, it
is the differences in conception which define Conrad's distinctive
view of Nothingness. In 'Caves' Forster animates the ascetic
tendency within India's diverse philosophies as an antique and
still practised way of perceiving the phenomenal world, one which
acknowledges that it has empirical validity but denies that it has
value. By juxtaposing this rigorously exclusive sensibility with the
joining of poetry and pragmatism in 'Mosque' and the world-
embracing mysticism of 'Temple', Forster produced a triadic
structure incorporating a spectrum of alternatives to the dominant western mode of cognition, all of which challenge that system
of thought that had reached its apotheosis in the aggressive and
triumphalist philosophy of imperialism. For Conrad, however,
who saw deeper into the larger social consciousness of imperialism and had a firmer grasp of its historical dynamics, but who also
carried more of its emotional and mental luggage, the rejection of
the world of empirical being and the willing dissolution of an
autonomous self in pursuit of an unspecified transcendence was
neither a possible nor a desirable means of reintegrating the
unconscious and intuitive aspects of mind with other faculties, but
a descent into the void. All the same, in the contrast between the
disposition of the activist, combative Lingard, stirred to pit his
will against the passive lands of the East, and the quest for
detachment from the priorities of the turbulent secular world,
incipient in both D'Alcacer and Jörgenson and embodied in
Balarab, *The Rescue* does intimate an alternative to the performance principle at the heart of modern western civilisation.
Whereas the narrative commentary, in its concern to demonstrate
the baleful consequences of 'sublime indifference', chides
D'Alcacer's secret aloofness from the life of man, denounces
Jörgenson's 'unearthly detachment' from the passions of earth
and castigates the ascetic, melancholy and hesitating warrior
chief, Balarab, for his 'mystic contempt for Allah's creation . . .

his mistrust of the universe' (p. 434), his late discovery of 'a passionate craving for security and peace' (p. 113),[23] these anticipate but are peripheral to the central dramatisation of Lingard's fall out of the world and into a mysterious current sweeping him to that torpor and self-forgetfulness which is the willed goal of asceticism but which engulfs him against his will and betokens an instinctual escape from action to inertia.

For a writer who expressed aversion for states of mysticism, rapture and exaltation,[24] and registered his recoil by testifying to ecstasy as the negation of consciousness and not its transcendence, Conrad was able to illuminate the lived reality of transport with a lucidity that moderates the inscribed depreciation:

> He had lost touch with the world . . . He had no thought. He was in the state of a man who, having cast his eyes through the open gates of Paradise, is rendered insensible by that moment's vision to all the forms and matters of the earth; and in the extremity of his emotion ceases even to look upon himself but as the subject of a sublime experience which exalts or unfits, sanctifies or damns – he didn't know which . . .

> It seemed to Lingard that he had been awake ever since he could remember. It was as to being alive that he felt not so sure. He had no doubt of his existence; but was this life – this profound indifference, this strange contempt for what his eyes could see, this distaste for words, this unbelief in the importance of things and men? He tried to regain possession of himself, his old self which had things to do, words to speak as well as to hear. But it was too difficult. He was seduced away by the tense feeling of existence far superior to the mere consciousness of life, and which in its immensity of contradictions, delight, dread, exultation and despair could not be faced and yet was not to be evaded. There was no peace in it. But who wanted peace? Surrender was better, the dreadful ease of slack limbs in the sweep of an enormous tide and in a divine emptiness of mind. If this was existence then he knew that he existed. (pp. 415, 431–2)

Although Lingard's state of Nirvana mimics the fiction's vista on the pristine, inert and isolated cosmos of the archipelago, it is not to its 'unconscious genius' or to the 'fascination of the primitive' that he succumbs but to the 'profound and amazing sensation' induced by sexual passion. Yet in the suspension of rational faculties, the sense that mere life is vanity, the resignation of the 'fierce power of his personality' for immersion in an oceanic embrace, Lingard's quiescence embodies a philosophical stance that the fiction attributes to the East as its dominant mode and ultimate goal, and if this is contemplated with some equanimity in the text, it is finally censured for being a perversion of human purpose since Lingard's mystical enlightenment is shown not only to arrest his power to act, but to obscure his perception of moral obligations in the secular world.[25]

Because the colonial landscape is transformed into a figure of an archaic, mindless and static cosmos, the fiction is situated within the territory mapped by the imperialist imagination. All the same *The Rescue* is itself a critical reflection on the very psychology it illuminates, not only registering, although without endorsing, alternatives to its culturally conditional myopia, but distancing itself from that form of consciousness which is blind to the authenticity of the other, and by translating it into recognisable form, misinterprets its 'truths'. If the pathetic fallacy travesties nature by assigning it human emotions and thoughts, then the colonial imagination distorts the alien world by denying it human qualities, rendering the people as icons and their circumstances as metaphysical signs. It is Mrs Travers, who had shocked the worldly D'Alcacer with her solipsistic inability to see anything in the world outside herself or to recognise any emotion except her own, who is the fiction's unseeing eye, rejecting the unknown as unknowable and defending her innermost self from any incursions. Disquietened by the foreign appearance and manners of Hassim and Immada, she converts them into mythical beings: 'The occurrences of the afternoon had been strange in themselves, but what struck her artistic sense was the vigour of their presentation. They outlined themselves before her memory with the clear simplicity of some immortal legend' (pp. 152–3). She edits the distant form of a man on the shore into 'an enigmatical figure in an Oriental tale with something weird and menacing in its sudden emergence and lonely progress' (p. 260); appraises a chieftain as she would an abstract design: 'He delighted Mrs Travers not as a living being but like a clever sketch in colours, a vivid rendering of an artist's version of some soul, delicate and fierce' (p. 297), and refuses what is intrinsic to the society she is observing by viewing its natural and human properties as the products of astonished western observation: 'It was still and empty to the naked eye and seemed to quiver in the sunshine like an immense painted curtain lowered upon the unknown . . . The lagoon, the beach, the colours and the shapes struck her more than ever as a luminous painting on an immense cloth hiding the movements of an inexplicable life' (pp. 260, 366). When danger obliges her momentarily to acknowledge the 'reality' of her environment, she soon reverts to denying what is before her: 'The opposite shore of the lagoon had resumed its aspect of a painted scene that would never roll up to disclose the truth behind its blinding and soulless splendour' (p. 369).

In the company of Malayans, she feels herself to be alone: 'The men with her were less than nothing. She could not speak to them; she could not understand them; the canoe might have been moving by enchantment' (p. 391), and she is careless of being observed by them: 'A million stars were looking on, too, and what did it matter? They were not of the world I know. And it is just the same with the eyes. They are not of the world I live in' (p. 400). Although susceptible to the gentle and destructive langour of the place, its silence and mysterious emptiness, its invitation to 'inward serenity' and 'peace without thought', she defends herself against its seduction by refusing to *see*: 'Was it land – land! It seemed to her even less palpable than a cloud, a mere sinister immobility above the unrest of the sea, nursing in its depth the unrest of men, who, to her mind, were no more real than fantastic shadows' (p. 247). To abstract these cognitions and sensations from the situation that gave them birth and read them as expressions of a transhistorical and supracultural alienation, would be to drain them of their intrinsic meanings, for these are articulations of the stranger from a dominant social order defending herself against the assaults of a foreign world she believes to be a negation of the norms and values that are her safety. The fiction's ambivalence towards Edith Travers – is she a bored and superficial adventuress hungry for a transient romantic interlude, or an adventurous spirit soaring above the restraints of her metropolitan existence? is she cynical and self-regarding or do her reprehensible acts stem from impeccable but ill-judged motives? – produces a dual perspective on her reactions where overt sympathy is extended to her misrecognitions and criticism

of her attenuated vision is oblique. But what the text does lay bare
is the process by which the western imagination constructs the
identity of the colonial world in terms that assign normality and
coherence to western modes and refuse the other for its failure to
conform to these canons.

In a letter sent to his American agent, J. B. Pinker, when the novel
was at last done, Conrad wrote: 'Novels of adventure will . . .
always be written; but it may well be that 'Rescue' in its
concentrated colouring and tone will remain the swan song of
Romance as a form of literary art'.[26] Here Conrad intimates one
source of the difficulties he had in writing a fiction where he set out
to rescue for posterity the memory of the colonial adventurer as
hero and, in looking back on the myths of a bygone age, came up
against evidence of baseness and disgrace which annihilated the
established usage of colonial romance. The first attempt at 'The
Rescuer' coincided with the start of work on *Heart of Darkness* and
Lord Jim, works which were to surpass the relatively simplistic
engagements with colonialism in *Almayer's Folly* and *An Outcast of
the Islands* and from which 'The Rescuer' was already beginning to
escape. The earlier writings can be read as illuminations of the
imperialist imagination rather than as critical reflections on the
corporate consciousness of imperialism, for the demystification of
colonialist benevolence is eclipsed by the mystification of the East
as a force of primal evil, a representation produced by the liberal
use of metaphors of stagnation, poison, decay, rottenness, corruption and death in tropical nature to signify not only human
propensities to depravity, but also 'the quagmire of barbarism' in
which the peoples of the archipelago are sunk. Such is the context
in which the encounter between West and East unfolds, where the
'corrupt' love that flares up between Malayan women and white
men is further vitiated by mutual incomprehension of each other's
motives, the inaccessibility of each other's minds, the hopeless
diversity of their two worlds, and is doomed to end in a hatred
born of race and blood. When a rhetoric resonant with racist
antipathy of the other is wrenched from the particular historical
circumstances it evokes and read as an articulation of generic
human isolation and loneliness, the effect is to neutralise the
fiction's fiercely partisan perspective on the Europeans' sense of
estrangement from the alien and conceal the empathy it extends

to the 'mysterious revolt' of heart, morality and intelligence against intimacy with the stranger.

It is from this unmoderated viewpoint that *The Rescue* distances itself, for although the exotic locations, arcane atmosphere, mysterious people and sensational topics native to popular fiction remain, the traditional forms of colonial romance are stretched and distorted to produce a critique of the ethos and perceptions such works authorised. By disappointing expectations, the novel signifies the exhaustion of a genre, since it disclaims the tenets of the colonialist creed to which it gives voice and delivers an elegy on a legend it had offered as a fit subject for eulogy. The yacht people are rescued and Lingard survives, but no one is 'saved'; of the cosmos the dishonoured Lingard had built around himself, nothing endures, nor can his kingdom bear the scrutiny of a backward look that sought manifestations of idealism but discovered signs of treachery. Conrad's letter to Pinker, who had asked him to provide a synopsis for *Cosmopolitan*, where it was hoped it would be serialised, is distinctly bitter: 'You may . . . assure the representative of the *Cosmopolitan Magazine* that the story will end as romantically as it began, and that no one of any particular consequence will have to die. Hassim and Immada will be sacrificed, as in any case they were bound to be, but their fate is not the subject of the tale. All those yacht people will go on their way, leaving Lingard alone with the wreck of the greatest adventure of his life'.[27]

4 *The Nigger of the 'Narcissus'*

When *Lord Jim* (1901) is read in conjunction with *The Nigger of the 'Narcissus'* (1897), the amalgam of defensive and subversive strategies in the later work stands out as an interrogation of the authoritarian philosophy which the earlier fiction underwrites. Both novels partake of received meanings and even in the ideologically heterodox *Lord Jim*, opposition to imperialism's world-outlook is deflected by the fiction's endorsement of patriotism as the noblest sentiment and ethnic solidarity as the ultimate loyalty. But crucial differences exist and these can be seen as a measure of Conrad's self-contradictory stance towards official ideas and values. Where the novella upholds the power to act, the longer fiction contemplates the faculty of visionary imagination, and where the first stands by the ethic of responsibility to socially appointed duties and excludes from its discussion further questions of the ends such action serves, the second reflects on the propriety of pursuing disentitled ideals at the expense of transgressing mores that govern the existing order. *The Nigger of the 'Narcissus'* militantly sponsors the commandment on 'law, order, duty and restraint, obedience, discipline' that had been hymned by Kipling and handed down as scripture to imperialism's servants, while *Lord Jim* considers the validity of heretical alternatives to imperialism's formal prescriptions. Whereas the one commends the virtues of compliant service practised by the masses of earlier days, the other looks towards the gratification of repressed desire and the realisation of idealistic intent. The declamatory narrative voice of the earlier work directs and cajoles the reader into accepting established customs as moral absolutes; the later fiction is on the other hand a sceptical meditation on the existence of 'a sovereign power enthroned in a fixed standard of conduct' which seeks to engage its audience in apprehending the variable and mutable status of ethical concepts and social laws.

If the first enjoins a solidarity that is narrowly defined as submission to the demands of a strictly regulated work community, the second makes an equivocal case for the faith and shadowy ideas of the gallant eccentric who is temperamentally unfitted for a subordinate role in the ranks. The one represents the outsider with anathema as a disease eroding the vigour of the corporate body, the other makes of the misfit its tarnished hero; the one excoriates compassion, sentimental pity and tenderness to suffering as capitulations to decadent egoism, the other is an exercise in an empathy forbidden by the social rules. The two works are marked by polarised attitudes to the idea of certainty, the first seeking to reclaim 'the certitude that lurks in doubts', the second recognising doubt as 'the inseparable part of our knowledge'. Where *The Nigger of the 'Narcissus'* denounces dissidence as a vice, mistrust of conventional wisdom is in *Lord Jim* displayed as the criterion of integrity, and the assumption advanced by the former that the standards of one segment of English society constitute universal moral categories, is in the latter the object of the fiction's scorn: 'Virtue is one all over the world, and there is only one faith, one conceivable conduct of life, one manner of dying' (p. 341). The interlocution in *Lord Jim* between stern voices pronouncing institutionalised beliefs to be unassailable truths, and the hesitant, tentative tones of a protagonist who is sensitive to the variety and mutability of doctrines and aspirations within a cultural formation, dramatises a conflict of incompatible social theories; in *The Nigger of the 'Narcissus'*, where the narrative mediators are lyrical about authorised deportment and venomous towards deviations, the central discussion is sealed from the challenge of dissenting viewpoints. Both fictions engage with the tension between the demands of the performance principle and the exigencies of unconscious need, but whereas the first indicts the impulse as degenerate and counsels restraint as necessary to the maintenance of the established régime, *Lord Jim* registers a protest against constraints on human faculties imposed to guarantee the stability of a repressive culture.

Through focusing exclusively on action for its own sake and as its own end, by acclaiming the sacredness of 'austere servitude' and declaring social obedience a moral imperative, *The Nigger of the 'Narcissus'* appears to be Conrad's most politically orthodox fiction and has been read as such by more than one critic. Jacques Berthoud, who dismisses 'the swarm of symbolic or allegorical interpretations that are now threatening to envelop Conrad's texts',[1] and argues for discovering meaning within what is written

in the fictions, offers a lucid analysis of the book's conscious levels:
in Berthoud's account, the fundamental question posed by the
work, how men's lives are justified, is answered by a narrative
which demonstrates 'that human existence is justified not by
words, but by deeds; not by demands, but by duties'.[2] This is a
coherent statement of the fiction's militantly presented theorem
but one that disregards the text's polyphonies, and because
neither the whole nor its subsidiary lemmas are proved in action
or discourse to be true, it is necessary to see how the argument of
the work's thesis is undercut and dissipated. For *The Nigger of the
'Narcissus'*, which does extol the old traditions of sea service and is
politically tendentious, is all the same not an unmodulated
affirmation of 'glorious and obscure toil', since it leaves in
suspension as many questions as it assertively answers, and what
is alluded to through signs and emblems is as charged with
contrary meanings as that which is orotund declamations is
averred. A title which is both expressly descriptive and implicitly
imagist, previews the fiction's heterogenous strategies and indicates that whereas the subject matter of this 'Tale of the Sea' is
'realistic', realism is not the novel's chosen mode. Conrad was not
convinced about the aptness of the name under which the work
was published, but with its juxtaposition of contrary symbols that
converge and bifurcate, it does happen to accommodate the
fiction's circuitous path around the antagonistic claims of
utilitarianism and unconscious desire. On the one hand the black
man, Wait, is the embodiment of death and the agency of that
'narcissistic' revolt against the tyranny of toil and renunciation –
that is, he is both Thanatos *and* Eros, and therefore absorbs both
possible connotations of the title's emblems into his person; on the
other hand, he, the 'Nigger', can be seen as representing the
antagonist to the tradition of action symbolised by a ship named
the *'Narcissus'*. The title thus not only condenses the images of
death and regression to quiescence, but registers an antinomy
that is structural to the fiction's undeclared dialogue, where the
satisfactions of existing within the 'reality' of the visible world, to
which the fiction is formally committed, must contend with
intimations of other longings, and the value of action categorically
endorsed by the text is undermined by omens of nature's
indifference to human purposes and threatened by mementoes of
mortality.

The fiction's resolute advocacy of the old merchant service, with its demands for duty, dedication and sacrifice, serves to sanction an anachronistic social mode still undisturbed by egalitarian ideas and socialist aspirations, and to this end the polemical disquisition is joined and enhanced by transfigurations of mundane artefacts and ordinary persons into apostolic figures incarnating the surpassing value of 'the tradition of the sea'.[3] Through kinetic montages, the hazardous life aboard a vessel returning with a cargo from the Far East is animated as a celebration of the joy of arduous labour: 'In an unendurable and unending strain they worked like men driven by a merciless dream to toil in an atmosphere of ice or flame' (pp. 92–3). The old practitioners of such exalted drudgery are perceived in their primordial essence as the rugged, uncultivated, strong and mute supports of culture and civilisation: 'they were effaced, bowed and enduring, like stone caryatides that hold up in the night the lighted halls of a resplendent and glorious edifice' (p. 25), and the living model of the single-minded fidelity, spiritual discipline and restraint that had characterised an earlier generation of seamen uncorrupted by and immune to subversive social doctrines, is the tried and tested old Singleton. With his white skin, white moustache and venerable white beard, he stands as the archetype of Service, 'a statue of heroic size in the gloom of the crypt' (p. 129), a promethean figure who illuminates the space he occupies: 'Singleton stood at the door with his face to the light and his back to the darkness. And alone in the dim emptiness of the sleeping forcastle he appeared bigger, colossal, very old' (p. 24). Thus through endowing obedient service with spiritual value, and equating renunciation with virtue, the pragmatic function of work in maintaining a particular mode of production and its associated social arrangements is suppressed and in vilifying other forms of labour relationships, the archaic forms of the merchant navy are accorded the status of a fixed moral principle by a text that resolutely advances an ideological representation of life at sea.[4]

In a fiction where the collective protagonist, the crew, fails to live up to the stringent codes of the sea, it is the ship, refusing the burden of a name given her by men, that rises above her material shape as an instrument of trade, to stand as the novel's heroine, its symbol of valour and endurance, and her passage from the unpolluted ocean which gives her life, to a grave on the adulterated earth, signposts the spiritual inequalities between the

ocean irradiated by a great light and the profound darkness of the
shore:

> an impure breeze shrieked a welcome between her stripped
> spars; and the land, closing in, stepped between the ship and
> the sea . . . Long drifts of smoky vapours soiled it with livid
> trails; it throbbed to the beat of millions of hearts, and from it
> came an immense and lamentable murmur – the murmur of
> millions of lips praying, cursing, sighing, jeering – the undying
> murmur of folly, regret, and hope exaled by the crowds of the
> anxious earth. The *Narcissus* entered the cloud . . . came gently
> into her berth; the shadows of soulless walls fell upon her, the
> dust of all the continents leaped upon her deck, and a swarm of
> strange men, clambering up her sides, took possession of her in
> the name of the sordid earth. She had ceased to live. (pp. 163–4,
> 165)

Impure, vapours, soiled, livid, obscene lamentations, anxious,
soulless, sordid – such words are intended to disparage a
quotidian contemporary world in the grip of base instincts, just as
the use of swarm and dust are calculated to insult the working
population of the shore, and the denigration, although couched in
recondite terms, is directed against the social condition of
England from where the process of class struggle and the influence
of libertarian ideas reach out to threaten the hierarchy still intact
in the community of the sea.

It is in this context that the ideological function of the sea within
the fiction's argument can be seen: as a physical entity, a highway
to trade and an actual place of work for mariners, it is
transubstantiated as the tangible, visible form of the unknown
and overarching cosmos: great, immortal, omniscient, terrible,
heartless, insatiable, mysterious, impenetrable, unintelligible,
incorruptible, unresting and infinite, the ocean is evoked through
superlatives and made sentient, a metaphysical power to be
addressed with fear, awe and reverence:

> The problem of life seemed too voluminous for the narrow
> limits of human speech, and by common consent it was
> abandoned to the great sea that had from the beginning
> unfolded it in its immense grip; to the sea that knew all, and
> would in time infallibly unveil to each the wisdom hidden in all

the errors, the certitude that lurks in doubts, the realm of safety
and peace beyond the frontiers of sorrows and fear . . . And the
immortal sea stretched away, immense and hazy, like the image
of life, with a glittering surface and lightless depths. (pp. 138,
155)[5]

If the cumulative effect of the multifarious epithets is to obscure
the ineffable attributes they are designed to illuminate, then the
intention of transmuting the sea into the consummate image of
those absolutes in which the human condition must bathe and
which regulate and temper its state, is all the same apparent. For
the sea is made to fulfil a sacerdotal purpose, pre-empting the role
of religion by delivering those elected to serve her from the accidie
which would otherwise be the species' earthly fate, inspiring
humankind to reach after distant and unseen goals: 'On men
reprieved by its disdainful mercy, the immortal sea confers in its
justice the full privilege of desired unrest. Through the perfect
wisdom of its grace they are not permitted to meditate at ease
upon the complicated and acrid flavour of existence' (p. 90).
The obverse of this tribute to the divine discontent engendered by
the sea is the call to social conformity implicit in the form of
service required by the merchant navy of a colonial power, and
both are conflated in the teaching that renunciation brings
fulfilment and that the road to spiritual freedom passes through
social submission. The fiction's homage to the standards of a
bygone age epitomised in the tradition of the sea reaches its
apotheosis in an address to England's old colonial might where
the island itself, as if freed from the taint of an earthly incarnation
and an existence in contemporary history, is evoked in the image
of a ship eternally fixed in time past:

A great ship! For ages had the ocean battered in vain her
enduring sides; she was there when the world was vaster and
darker, when the sea was great and mysterious, and ready to
surrender the prize of fame to audacious men. A ship mother of
fleets and nations! The great flagship of the race; stronger than
the storms! and anchored in the open sea. (p. 163)

Thus do the fiction's images, emblems and imitations converge on
illuminating the sea as the source and agency of those habits
necessary to the continuance of the old order, the one calling on

humankind to strive after inner perfection, the other instilling the ways of public obedience, both commanding self-abnegation, refusing political rebellion and acting to reconcile imperialism's servants to the toil and sacrifice of their lowly but sublime role. It is therefore the sea, the incarnation of the infinitudes of space and time, that is pressed into service as the fiction's instrument of the performance principle, the voice of established morality and the regulator of the ego's energies.

Because the narrative mediation is divided between an anonymous, uncharacterised protagonist recounting events he had witnessed, and an omniscient narrator whose commentary does not depart from the ideological premises this voice advances – the text moves freely and impartially between the 'we' of the one and the 'they' of the other – the articulation of an aggressive polemic on the morality of blind faith, forebearance and obedience to duty, is undisputed. Within the structure of a sea adventure told as a conservative political allegory, the themes of solidarity and anomie, order and anarchy, obedience and rebellion, are engaged and controlled from the standpoint of authoritarian thought, and since the tale is related as a confession by a participant who, although using a syntax distinct from the argot of his unschooled shipmates, had been a crew-member on that fateful voyage, his self-castigating and sententious delivery has the authority of a lived experience that has brought him wisdom and earned him the right to pontificate. The social milieu that produced him, to which he owes allegiance and for which he speaks, is made evident in an idiom he shares with the officers, a delivery replete with words like 'grit', 'unmanly lie' and 'guileless manhood', and inflated by the patriotic oratory and rose-hued recollections of Home that were obligatory in every colonial romance:

> Young Creighton stood leaning over the rail, and looked dreamily into the night of the East. And he saw in it a long country lane, a lane of waving leaves and dancing sunshine. He saw stirring boughs of old trees outspread, and framing in their arch the tender, the caressing blueness of an English sky. And through the arch a girl in a light dress, smiling under a sunshade, seemed to be stepping out of the tender sky. (pp. 21–2)

Such expressions of nostalgia, which were an essential element in the subculture of the British Service Classes exiled to the colonies, serve to place the narrator, and from the stronghold of the political conservatism where this group sought refuge, he launches an assault on those who would subvert the established social arrangements – an agitator born in the slums of England and a colonial malingerer, an attack which calumniates the visionary aspiration and large goals of movements for social change and gives free rein to xenophobia.

The diatribes against Donkin, a crude caricature of a mean, cowardly, incompetent, unprincipled, parasitic, spiteful, ill-spoken and physically repellent guttersnipe, who is, absurdly, the fiction's avatar of socialist ideas, are directed at the 'filthy eloquence' of his seditious appeals to equality, rights, justice and exploitation. With 'the white skin of his limbs showing his human kinship through the black fantasy of his rags' (p. 12), Donkin is a source of disruption from within the ship's racially homogeneous if culturally various universe, who undermines the stability of the community by awakening a sense of grievance in men who despise him but identify with the discontent he articulates, an unrest crudely traduced by the text: 'and inspired by Donkin's hopeful doctrines they dreamed enthusiastically of the time when every lonely ship would travel over a serene sea, manned by a wealthy and well-fed crew of satisfied skippers' (p. 103). If the vile Donkin is conceived as an internal agent of political disruption, then the black sailor is isolated as a minatory visitation from another galaxy, perceived by one of the crew as the corporeal form of the devil, represented by the narrative commentary as a daemonic intermediary casting an 'infernal spell' over the men and the elements, and present in the fiction as the incarnation of the unreconstructed Id and the death instinct.

In the moral triangle which the fiction maps, the Titanic figure of Singleton, relic of an age untouched by individualism and socialism, stands at the apex with his two adversaries, Donkin and Wait, at the bases, and in this space dominated by the three protagonists the battle for the soul of the crew is fought, a struggle of obedience against disaffection in the social realm, and an ontological contest between the demands of the empirical world and the desire to escape from its pressures. The living witness to fortitude and faithfulness in the one conflict and the representative of the 'reality' tenet in the other, is characterised as without thought or vision, doubt or hope, a man speechless and drained of emotion: 'He stood, still strong, as ever unthinking; a ready man with a vast, empty past and with no future, with his childlike impulses and his man's passions already dead within his tattooed breast' (pp. 24–5).

The fiction's focus on Singleton is calculated to win the reader's consent to the majestic stature conferred on him, and this device is at its most seductive in the presentation of the old sailor standing firm and alert amidst the havoc of a storm:

> Swaying upon the din and tumult of the seas, with the whole battered length of the ship launched forward in a rolling rush before his steady old eyes, he stood rigidly still, forgotten by all, and with an attentive face. In front of his erect figure only the two arms moved crosswise with a swift and sudden readiness, to check or urge again the rapid stir of circling spokes. He steered with care. (p. 89)

It is apparent that Conrad intended his audience to see in Singleton an exemplary and wholly admirable being; all the same the meanings immanent in this representation are not as unambiguous as many critics and in particular Ian Watt would have an audience accept:

> Conrad's sudden and drastic narrowing of the narrative horizon brings home our utter, but usually forgotten, dependence, on the labors of others. To make us see the ultimate and universal basis of human solidarity Conrad has reserved his greatest art to make us pause at the spectacle of a man who steers with care . . . There is surely a special moral for readers and critics here: for, in making us look up to Singleton at the wheel, Conrad compels us, in a humbling moment of awed vision, to acknowledge our solidarity with those who cannot write and who read only Bulwer-Lytton.[6]

But not all readers in this or any other age would necessarily agree to such an interpretation as canonical since this requires belief in the ethic of means, acceptance of a form of solidarity that is inseparable from the mechanics of political domination and which demands of its servants that they neither write nor speak, think nor doubt, and assent to the repression of those instincts and wants that interfere with the execution of prescribed functions in an oppressive society. Nor is the victory of Singleton's renunciations and inhibitions unchallenged since the fiction's central drama is concentrated on the revolt against the culture of toil and sacrifice. It can therefore be argued that some audiences will see in Singleton not a paradigm of moral excellence but a living condition of blind obedience and psychic constraint, and that he will appear to them unsavoury not because he is a stranger to high culture but because he obeys orders without concern for the goals these serve and has connived in the suppression of whole areas of his being.

To claim as some critics have done that Conrad successfully establishes the driving of the ship as the sole and proper principle of action, is to overlook the fiction's unacknowledged political matrix, for the ship is in passing designated as an instrument of colonial trade ['The august loneliness of her path lent dignity to the sordid inspiration of her pilgrimage' (p. 30)], the inescapable implication of which is that the steering of the *Narcissus* does have an end that the text shuts off from view. Because of this exclusion, the acting out of the moral conflict produces an overt political statement cramped and confined by the anxieties of a segment within or on the margins of the dominant class, sustained by belief in their indispensable function, threatened by alternatives to their ethos and fearful of changes that would undermine their privileged reason for being. The visionary historical dimension that was to expand in Conrad's subsequent political fictions from within the framework of a conservative ideology is therefore absent; instead, the challenge to the official viewpoint comes from outside the province of formal political thought and is lodged in the ontological argument about the value of action and the absolute rule of utilitarianism. With the arrival of a moribund West Indian, 'the casual St. Kitts' nigger' uprooted from his own society and indifferent to the codes of the merchant navy he had opportunistically joined, who flaunts, exploits and denies his condition, Singleton's age-old victory against doubt, fear and desire is shown to be at risk and battle is poised between the forces of light probity and 'reality' and darkness, deceit and Nirvana. Or so it would seem, for the loading of the moral scales in Singleton's favour is unbalanced by the weight of human and mythic qualities, positive and negative, conferred on the black man: he is proud and craven, appealing and disgusting, a menacing interloper intruding on an integral community with 'his awful and veiled familiar', and a majestic presence who exerts an unspecified authority over the men of the *Narcissus*. The juxtaposition of the two words, one an offensive racist term,[7] used to single out a black sailor, the other a name attached to a symbol of the practice of toil but ineradicably associated with the legend of the youth who bequeathed a diametrically opposed tradition devoted to peace, rest and inertia, registers the dual and disjunctive implications of the title. For the fiction not only dramatises the conflict between the morbid and the vital, and between quiescence and performance, but overturns expectations of how the confrontation will be enacted, since the black man as well as inducing revulsion commands respect,[8] and the white crew of the *Narcissus* prove to be something less than exemplars of austere and sacrificial service.

It is made evident at Wait's first appearance that paradoxical responses of awe and abhorrence, pity and hatred, are to be invited:

> The nigger was calm, cool, towering, superb. The men had approached and stood behind him in a body. He overtopped the tallest by half a head. He said: 'I belong to the ship'. He enunciated distinctly, with soft precision. The deep rolling tones of his voice filled the deck without effort. He was naturally scornful, unaffectedly condescending, as if from his height of six foot three he had surveyed all the vastness of human folly and had made up his mind not to be too hard on it ... The disdainful tones had ceased, and, breathing heavily, he stood still, surrounded by all these white men. He held his head up in the glare of the lamp – a head vigorously modelled into deep shadows and shining lights – a head powerful and misshapen with a tormented and flattened face – a face pathetic and brutal: the tragic, the mysterious, the repulsive mask of a nigger's soul. (p. 18)

The antinomies contained in this passage rehearse Wait's incompatible roles in the fiction, and both the odium directed at the temerity of a black man who confronts a gathering of whites without deference and the racist recoil expressed at his unfamiliar physical features are more than overwhelmed by the perception of his transcendent stature. He is death conceived as the eternal, implacable and intolerable destiny of all living things: 'He seemed to hasten the retreat of departing light by his very presence; the setting sun dipped sharply, as though fleeing before our nigger; a black mist emanated from him; a subtle and dismal influence; a something cold and gloomy that floated out and settled on all the faces like a mourning veil' (p. 34); and he is the very form of memento mori, the traditional death's head of Christian cultures, fashioned to recall the living to thoughts of their sins, their failings and their mortality, and therefore a salutary image: 'He was becoming immaterial like an apparition; his cheekbones rose, the forehead slanted more; the face was all hollows, patches of shade; and the fleshless head resembled a disinterred black skull, fitted with two restless globes of silver in the sockets of his eyes' (p. 139).

His sonorously spoken first words, 'I belong to the ship' state the incontrovertible fact that death is ubiquitous and inexorable, a truth confirmed by the text's sequence of mortuary images – the men's berths seen as narrow niches for coffins in a whitewashed and lighted morgue, 'like graves tenanted by uneasy corpses' (p. 22), the forecastle at night as quiet as a sepulchre – and the allusions made by both Singleton and the sailmaker, whose hated job it is to sew shrouds, to death's permanent presence at sea. However, in pursuit of proving the case for a martial form of solidarity that disallows the self-indulgence of compassion, the text departs from the sober recognition of this biological certainty and concentrates instead on upbraiding the degenerative effects on the crew of Wait's refusal to consent to his death:

> Falsehood triumphed. It triumphed through doubt, through stupidity, through pity, through sentimentalism . . . The latent egoism of tenderness to suffering appeared in the developing anxiety not to see him die . . . He was demoralising. Through him we were becoming highly humanised, tender, complex, excessively decadent: we understood the subtlety of his fear, sympathised with all his repulsions, shrinkings, evasions, delusions – as though we had been overcivilised, and rotten, and without any knowledge of the meaning of life. (pp. 138, 139)

Yet the flow of abuse directed against Wait because he is unwilling to emulate the fatalistic acceptance of death advocated by a Singleton is not only arrested by gestures of sympathy for the plight of the black man dying far from home but, against the grain of its jeremiads on his baleful and unwholesome presence, the fiction rescues him from the ignominious role in which he had been cast to show in him a positive image of Nirvana, of death not as destruction but transfigured into the form of rest and silence: 'He was scornful and brooding; he looked ahead upon the sea, and no one could tell what was the meaning of that black man, sitting apart in a meditative attitude and as motionless as a carving' (p. 45). That it is a black man from a distant foreign land who is the fiction's bearer of the death instinct, of the impulse to escape the turbulence of the empirical world and return to the primordial inertia of the inorganic realm, suggests the intrusion of an alien and unwelcome mode into the fiction's approved 'reality', and this indictment is delivered by narrative voices denouncing social rebellion and instinctual gratification from an ideological plinth. But what the fiction *shows* in the corporate behaviour of the crew is men turning away from the hardships of toil and oppression and towards release from tension and pressure, a move that signals the failure of the promise that surrender to 'the sea' will assuage desire. Ultimately Wait towers more than physically over men who are robbed of certainty about the value of their endeavours and the rewards of their deprivations, for contending with the fiction's persistent obloquy at his manner of dying is the acknowledgement that the company of the *Narcissus* is transformed by his silent prophecy of an alternative tendency inimical to the tradition of the sea. Wait is despised and rejected as a liar and a coward but the impact of this abuse is deflected by the weight of this presence as a mythical being who arouses in the crew the impulse for easeful death, the urge to withdraw from the pressures of exertion and enter into long rest, dark death and dreamful ease.

The *Preface* written to accompany the work when it was first published and renowned amongst critics as a manifesto of literary impressionism, is deserving of notice for designing emblems of hope which the text signally fails to fly. The artist, Conrad writes, speaks 'to the latent feeling of fellowship with all creation – and to the subtle but invincible conviction of solidarity that knits together the loneliness of innumerable hearts', and seeks to awaken 'in the hearts of the beholders that feeling of unavoidable solidarity; of the solidarity in mysterious origin, in toil, in joy, in hope, in uncertain fate, which binds men to each other and all mankind to the visible world' (pp. viii, x). The universal embrace of these sublime sentiments, the optimism further uplifted by the testimony of the *Epigraph*, '. . . My Lord in his discourse discovered a great deal of love to this ship', and reiterated in the text's high-flown eloquence on the 'brotherhood of the sea' united by 'the exacting appeal of the work', the 'courage . . . endurance . . . the unexpressed faith . . . the unspoken loyalty that knits together a ship's company' (p. 11), promises a tale that will demonstrate this ennobling fellowship. Instead, competing with and undercutting the eulogies to the ideal, is a relentless denunciation of the actual body that serves to incarnate the abstract concept. For what is shown is a precarious state of fragile unity gained and lost amongst a vacillating group of decent but susceptible men possessed by 'vague and burning desires', who are brave and generous but wanting in sustained moral courage, are capable of withstanding hardships but prone to flaccidity, are united impartially by the recognition of necessity and the sentimental lie, are moved to acts of valour and swayed by specious emotion, are made mutinous by subversive propaganda and cowed by the proper exercise of authority.

These then are the 'children of the discontented earth', a generation exposed to new concepts of rights, justice and liberty and seduced away from the devotion to duty that had characterised 'the everlasting children of the mysterious sea' (p. 25). The crew of the *Narcissus* is thus shown to be a contemporary and alienated workforce, bound by rules rather than conviction, a random group of men trained to obedience, overseen by officers skilled in command and hired to navigate a merchant vessel engaged in colonial trade, a community within which sporadic camaraderie will be engendered but which is remote from the ecumenical conception of fellowship envisioned in the Preface. It is because the men of the *Narcissus* constitute a temporary and loose association held together by discipline and hierarchy and not a fraternity of persons autonomously come together in pursuit of a shared goal, joined by common beliefs and inspired by a dream of the future, that dissension and near-mutiny during the voyage appears as a structural fault rather than an accidental catastrophe and their dispersal at the journey's end inevitable.[9] If the idea of solidarity advanced in the *Preface* suggests a spiritual realm within whose circle personal death would be freed of fear and the vain hope of a subjective tomorrow freely forfeited for the

eternal life of contributing to a collective destiny, then the text in
its draconian insistence on death as an individual ordeal to be
stoically endured displays its absence in the fiction's world.
Indeed the irate narrator articulates moral revulsion at the crew's
sentimental identification with the black man's affliction which is
an expression of their own desire to retreat from the weariness, the
fever and the fret of their daily existence: 'They clustered around
that morbid carcass, the fit emblem of their aspirations' (p. 122);
and it is the fiction's exemplar of the cardinal virtues in the
Protestant-capitalist canon who condemns Wait to a solitary
death, his sentence joining racist indifference for the stricken
person with dispassionate assent to the universal necessity, a
construction that negates the boundless ideal of the *Preface* and
affirms the text's representation of a solidarity in uniform: 'Are
you dying? . . . Well, get on with your dying . . . don't raise a
blamed fuss with us over that job. We can't help you . . . And a
black fellow, too . . . I have seen them die like flies . . . You can't
help him; die he must' (pp. 42, 129, 130).

The disarray of the arguments the fiction set out to prove, and
the proven disjunction between the infinite aspiration it pursues
and the small possibility it acknowledges, reveal the fate of fixed
theological premises when exposed to perceptions of a changing
social condition. Even as the discourse lauds the ontological
exhilaration of submitting to the travail of a servitude that offers
only its own reward, the action demonstrates a contemporary
state in which such recompense is neither available nor sought,
and against this disenchanted awareness that the tradition to
whose adulation the work is committed has lost its social base, the
vaunting optimism of the last pages, where the images of the
sordid earth, its material interests and ignoble people, are
momentarily transfigured into figures of promise, stands out as a
symbolic gesture to a victory that cannot be won but must be
honoured:

> The sunshine of heaven fell like a gift of grace on the mud of the
> earth, on the remembering and mute stones, on greed, on
> selfishness; on the anxious faces of forgetful men. And to the
> right of the dark group, the stained front of the Mint, cleansed
> by the flood of light, stood out for a moment dazzling and white
> like a marble palace in a fairy tale. The crew of the *Narcissus*
> drifted out of sight . . . Haven't we, together and upon the

immortal sea, wrung out a meaning from our sinful lives? Good-bye, brothers! You were a good crowd. As good a crowd as ever fisted with wild cries the beating canvas of a heavy foresail; or tossing aloft, invisible in the night, gave back yell for yell to a westerly gale. (pp. 172, 173)

The challenge to the fiction's overt political meanings, stridently and sentimentally declared in a rhetoric that leaves no space for the development of an internal dialogue, is engendered from within the discontinuous mythopoeic mode, and it is as a counter-attack on this subversion that the final encomium is nakedly offered.

5 *Lord Jim*

Conrad's reference to *Lord Jim* as a free and wandering tale may seem an improbable description of a work that unsparingly engages with the ideological origins and political uses of moral precepts, but it is suggestive of the generous and inquiring outlook produced by the novel's expansive narrative structure. Within the matrix of the fiction's polymorphous discourse, an ethical debate between the sanctions upholding conventional mores and the entitlement of heterodox postures, and in which both sides assume the legitimacy of the given social order, is interpenetrated and transcended by an enveloping ontological discussion where the drive for an alternative condition is articulated and the idea of a differently constructed culture projected. Thus a consciousness fixed on problems of conduct within the existing social world meets with the utopian aspiration after realising other forms of value, and the visible triumphs of the performance principle are dwarfed by the hopes of the visionary imagination. The effect of this dialogue is to interrogate a range of assumptions fundamental to the official ethos; however, this tendency is arrested when the text legitimises imperialism's formal suppositions by locating the source of moral consciousness in obedience to the spirit of a mystically conceived homeland and seeking to identify the saving impulses redeeming a heartless and conscienceless project.

To this extent the novel remains connected with the dominant mode of thought; where it stands on independent ground is in revealing the concealed premises of imperialism's philosophical foundations, moral injunctions and authorised ways of seeing, for that which in *The Nigger of the 'Narcissus'* is consigned to the periphery of the fiction's vista and disallowed by the terms of its colloquy, is the subject of mediation in *Lord Jim* – the political functions of moral absolutes, the mutability of fixed standards, the urgent claims of natural impulses, the case for regarding the pursuit of an ideal condition as a spiritual imperative. When Marlow speaks out for those 'moments of awakening' that

76

transform consciousness, he delivers a protest against the repression of sensibility and the atrophy of vision which in *The Nigger of the 'Narcissus'* would have resounded as a call to rebellion, eliciting the execrations of the narrative voices and causing Marlow to be cast in the role of a seditious intruder. This affirmation of areas of experience disparaged by the other work is transmuted in the dichotomous imagery of light and dark where the sunshine displays the meanings acquired through rational cognition, and the dim light of moon and stars illuminates the realms of unconscious being, and if Marlow in conformity with his inherited beliefs and professional training denigrates the last for giving 'a sinister reality to shadows alone' (p. 246), he also, when analysing his paradoxical response to Jim, endorses the necessity of embracing both domains: 'He appealed to all sides at once – to the side turned perpetually to the light of day, and to that side of us which, like the other hemisphere of the moon, exists stealthily in perpetual darkness' (p. 93). It is this rejection of the severance between reason and instinct, thought and feeling, that is transfigured in the protean form of Patusan's hills which from one aspect appear separated by a deep fissure and from another can be seen to be a single formation split in two by a narrow ravine 'with the two halves leaning slightly apart' (p. 220).[1]

Yet any interpretation of the novel as a univocal critique of imperialist ideology[2] must overlook the multiple and incompatible meanings that can be constructed from a text which dramatises the conflicting demands of constraint and freedom, conformity and individual conscience, responsibility to the laws of order and progress and fidelity to an unlicensed visionary faith, allegiance to tradition and commitment to a restructured future. In the absence of one omniscient viewpoint the interlocution of narrative voices constitutes the fiction's organising principle, and within the development of the moral and philosophical arguments, the eponymous anti-hero who, although he neither originates an alternative ethic nor incarnates the utopian imagination yet generates discussion of both, is the object of speculation rather than a participating intelligence. Through the perceptions of other protagonists who act as his judges or confessors, his motives and actions are expounded from a spectrum of subjective positions on matters of theory and belief, so that what Jim *is*, and the fiction is concerned to present him as an enigma to be decoded through the exercise of an innovatory system of analysis, is not the

same as how he is seen, and it is how he is seen that is of
significance. This distinction between his opaque essence and his
apprehensible image is conceded by the scrupulous Marlow, who
apologises to his audience for telling them so much about his own
'instinctive feelings and bemused reflections': 'He existed for me,
and after all it is only through me that he exists for you' (p. 224).
Such an admission of a personal and therefore qualified perception of Jim contrasts with the ostensibly objective record of Jim's
origins, history and present circumstances provided by the first
and anonymous narrator, whose introduction, despite the air of
reliable detachment it affects, turns out to be enmeshed with
prejudice.

Although like Marlow he can speak cynically about the clergy
as the officially appointed custodians of morality whose function it
is to manipulate piety and faith as a means of social control ['Jim's
father possessed such certain knowledge of the Unknowable as
made for the righteousness of people in cottages without disturbing the ease of mind of those whom an unerring Providence
enables to live in mansions' (p. 5)], he looks on Jim's person and
situation from the standpoint of one who consents to the
imposition of regulations that will ensure the uniformity, cohesion
and equilibrium of existing social arrangements. For him Jim's
failure to acquire 'perfect love of work' and his passing infatuation
with the Eastern promise of eternal peace, is evidence of a moral
flaw that separates him from those of his own kind who had been
successfully moulded by discipline, and from the pilgrims sustained by an austere and exacting faith and whose trust he
betrays. His derision of Jim's hunger for the unattainable is
spoken as a warning on the dangers of imagination and the fatal
distraction of longing for the ideal, and his admonition of Jim's
failure to comply with an established norm of conduct makes no
assessment of the premises or purposes of that code. All the same
his sententious version of a problematic situation allows that
there is more to Jim's case than can be explained by the 'facts' the
official Inquiry demands, and when he hands the narration over
to Marlow, it is an acknowledgement that his outlook is insufficient for a task that requires other ways of seeing. Thus despite
this narrator's privileged role as the first voice, his choral function
is undeveloped and he speaks merely as one of a group of
communicants adhering to ratified views and therefore expressing
adverse opinions about Jim, and whose composite image of him is

subtly and irrevocably altered by the substance of Marlow's
mediation.

If the opening out of a wide perspective on Jim allows for many
angles of vision, then both his critics and his protectors agree that
he is an outsider by temperament and not an outlaw by
conviction, a misfit rather than a rebel, who despite estrangement
from his immediate family and displacement amongst the larger
body of the merchant navy, is recognisably the product of
imperialism's Service Classes. His idiom is reminiscent of a Boy
Scout, his demeanour that of a disgraced subaltern eager for the
chance to prove his true worth, and the youthful dreams which
had set him apart from his more tractable companions on the
training ship are taken chapter and verse from popular colonial
fiction, retaining intact the veneration of endurance and leader-
ship native to the genre. Jim's fantasies of surpassing heroism
both ironically anticipate his abysmal failure and preview his
magnificent achievement, the first violating his nation's imperialist creed and the other realising its colonial dream, and it is
because he overturns expectations and blurs accepted discriminations by committing an iniquitous deed without himself being
vicious and while continuing to profess fidelity to the traditions he
has traduced, that he induces the reappraisal of old moral
certainties and stimulates the construction of other standards of
evaluation. It is Marlow's function to conduct this discussion, and
in his narration Marlow, an older and more disenchanted avatar
of the protagonist met with in *Heart of Darkness*, and one possessed
of greater self-awareness and a larger degree of self-doubt, enacts
his own passage from confidence in received ideas and authorised
values to an uneasy agnosticism about both.

What his exchanges with the other voices demonstrate, is a
passage fraught with doubts, hesitations and retreats, from
reliance on 'a few simple notions you must cling to if you want to
live decently and would like to die easy' (p. 43),[3] to a moral vision
cognisant of grey areas and intractable problems that customary
wisdom cannot even recognise:

> I felt the risk I ran of being circumvented, blinded, decoyed,
> bullied, perhaps, into taking a definite part in a dispute
> impossible of decision if one had to be fair to all the phantoms in
> possession – to the reputable that had its claims and to the
> disreputable that had its exigencies. I can't explain to you who

haven't seen him and who hear his words only at second hand
the mixed nature of my feelings. It seemed to me that I was
being made to comprehend the Inconceivable – and I know of
nothing to compare with the discomfort of such a sensation. I
was made to look at the convention that lurks in all truth and on
the essential sincerity of falsehood. (p. 93)

This passage with its finely balanced antinomies and deliberated
dissonances articulates Marlow's shock at recognising the arbit-
rariness of rigid moral categories and rehearses the essence of the
inadmissible evidence he is obliged to examine, testimony he is
initially predisposed to obfuscate and that ultimately colludes in
transforming his personal theology. At the outset inclined to join
in the general censure of Jim, whose improper professional
conduct threatens 'the honour of the craft' to which Marlow
belongs, and discomforted by a sense of 'the infernal alloy in his
metal', 'the subtle unsoundness' of one who would put his
disgrace before his guilt, Marlow is at the same time drawn to
Jim's familiar and congenial features: 'I liked his appearance; I
knew his appearance; he came from the right place; he was one of
us' (p. 43).

It is a measure of Marlow's re-education that what he comes to
value in Jim are those qualities at variance with his outward
image as the very model of colonial manhood – his romantic
conscience, his innocent individualism, his yearnings after an
ideal, and in allowing that the two 'jumps' marking the definitive
discontinuities in Jim's history were not the results of conscious
will and rational decision ['I had jumped . . . It seems . . . I knew
nothing about it until I looked up' (p. 111), is Jim's recollection of
leaving the ship, just as he remembers his flight from imprison-
ment in the Rajah's compound and to the safety of Doramin's
Settlement as having been executed 'without any mental process
as it were' (p. 253)], and that cowardice does not adequately
describe the one nor courage the other, Marlow is himself
transported to a new vantage point from which he can command a
wider view of the mainsprings to human action and exercise a
greater tolerance of deviations from the statutory norm. Although
Marlow is the fiction's principal narrator and its central intelligence, his viewpoint is itself the subject of scrutiny, and as a voice
that is both sardonic and earnest, self-deprecating and self-
righteous, Marlow acts not only as the communicator of the text's

unquiet conscience about 'fixed standards', but as the means through which the remaking of a consciousness is revealed. As Marlow defies and submits to 'the power of merciless convention', defends the exigencies of the disreputable and advances the claims of the reputable, so does his struggle with the prerogatives of antagonistic principles and the pull of contradictory feelings introduce inconsistencies into his testimony and exegesis.[4]

In a novel which has as its *Epigraph* the quotation 'It is certain my conviction gains infinitely the moment another soul will believe in it', uncertainty is the key-note of Marlow's address, one that seems calculated to involve his audience in his perplexity rather than to convert them to his now endangered convictions. His narration, in contradistinction to the official Inquiry which wants only facts, takes the form of an investigation into the credentials of those meanings and values morally binding on members of his social order, and since Marlow's findings discredit the postures of his complaisant interlocutors and imperil the tenets of his own persuasion, his delivery has need of oxymoron to communicate the sense of dislocation at finding no fixed and invariable points of reference, and confronting the necessity of inventing an alternative epistemology:

> I cannot say I had ever seen him distinctly . . . but it seemed to me that the less I understood the more I was bound to him in the name of that doubt which is the inseparable part of our knowledge . . . It was a strange and melancholy illusion, evolved half-consciously like all our illusions, which I suspect only to be visions of remote, unattainable truth, seen dimly . . . I have that feeling about me now; perhaps it is that feeling which has incited me to tell you the story, to try and hand over to you, as it were, its very existence, its reality – the truth disclosed in a moment of illusion. (pp. 221, 323)

Marlow's use of illusion to signify the prefiguration of a truth not yet grasped and not its negation, marks a departure from his accustomed habits of thought and registers an acknowledgement that the familiar vocabulary of empiricism is inadequate to comprehend the quality of his new perceptions. That the long-standing adherent of positivism finds himself reaching after 'absolute Truth, which, like Beauty itself, floats elusive, obscure, half-submerged, in the silent and still waters of mystery (p. 216),

and employs the language of metaphysics to register this ambition, intimates the dimensions of his crisis and suggests a context
for his concerted and elaborate mystification of Jim's person.

Since Jim's unspeakable act is not commensurate with his
appearance, manner, origins and training, Marlow spontaneously obscures that which he does see but cannot admit, and his
view of Jim observed through fog, haze and mist[5] registers the
opacity of his vision and not the intrinsic unintelligibility of the
person perceived: 'He was not – if I may say so – clear to me. He
was not clear . . . I cannot say I had ever seen him distinctly . . . I
am fated never to see him clearly . . . For me that white figure in
the stillness of the coast and sea seemed to stand at the heart of a
vast enigma' (pp. 177, 221, 241, 336). Inevitably Marlow, whose
sense of reality had hitherto derived from the assimilation of
observable facts and the recognition of unqualified moral distinctions, consigns Jim to a place in the crepuscular light; but when he
demands that attention be paid to Jim's 'shadowy ideal of
conduct', he is obliged to step outside 'the sheltering conception of
light and order which is our refuge' (p. 313) and allow that the
dark is an inseparable part of reality and not its annulment. In his
search for Jim's 'truth', Marlow negotiates a path through the
realms of empirical observation and intuitive insight, signposting
his route with images of sun and moon and designating positive
qualities to the first and negative properties to the other:

> There is something haunting in the light of the moon; it has all
> the dispassionateness of a disembodied soul, and something of
> its inconceivable mystery. It is to our sunshine, which – say
> what you like – is all we have to live by, what the echo is to the
> sound: misleading and confusing whether the note be mocking
> or sad. It robs all form of matter – which after all, is our domain
> – of their substance and gives a sinister reality to shadows
> alone. (p. 246)

All the same Marlow is troubled by what the dark holds ['What is
it that moves there?' he asks on gazing into a deep well', 'Is it a
blind monster or only a lost gleam from the universe?' (p. 307)],
and out of discontent with the conventional schema he still
continues to reiterate, he not only posits the light as a pragmatic
utility rather than a sign of an epistemological truth, a sanctuary
from 'the chaos of dark thoughts' that shuts off 'a view of a world

that seemed to wear a vast and dismal aspect of disorder' (p. 313), but rescues from disrepute and derogation the aspects of reality denied by his culture. Thus because Marlow is conceived as a protagonist able to distance himself from current orthodoxies and contemplate dissident alternatives, he is equipped by the fiction to do battle for the reputation of the outcast Jim and in doing so to interrogate an aspiration vilified by the official spokesmen of imperialist civilisation.

The debate between traditional values and heterodox ideals is dramatised in the course of Marlow's implicit dissociation from the negative evaluation made of Jim by the first narrator, and his direct confrontations with the doctrinaire views advanced by those protagonists whose unbending disavowal of the renegade obliges him to clarify the terms of his own eccentric allegiance. In the opinion of the skilled, courageous and ostensibly self-assured Captain Brierly, the epitome of Service and Honour, the disclosure of Jim's disgrace defames the public image of the maritime community and he wants nothing so much as that Jim should disappear, leaving the noble features of the merchant navy in pristine condition. Marlow can easily dispose of a stance dependent on keeping up formal appearances and devoid of moral content, and his bald and neutral reference to Brierly's suicide soon after the reported conversation draws attention to the fragility of the man's rigid adherence to a practice that is not rooted in moral conviction. Here Marlow discloses a shift in his own attitudes that serves to moderate his initial judgement of Jim, and by the time of his meeting with the French Lieutenant who had years earlier been a member of the boarding-party gone to the aid of the stricken *Patna*, Marlow had allied himself with Jim, while still seeking a sound basis for this commitment and needing reassurance on the fitness of his anomalous loyalty.

Hence he eagerly invites the stalwart old seaman, scarred by wounds that display past valour, possessed of an inert placidity and a dispassionate demeanour that speak of emotional restraint, to join him in taking a 'lenient view' of Jim's case, a miscalculation which obliges Marlow to witness the manner of his companion change from that of a tolerant village priest, accustomed to confessions of sin, suffering and remorse, to that of a cold and formal judge: 'He drew up his heavy eyelids . . . I was confronted by two narrow grey circlets, like two tiny steel rings around the profound blackness of the pupils. The sharp glance, coming from that massive body, gave a notion of extreme efficiency, like a razor-edge on a battle-axe' (p. 148). The dominant imagery of weaponry in Marlow's recollection establishes a connection between iron self-discipline and the repression of sensibility, and when the decent old sailor, to escape the discomfort of Marlow's outrageous suggestion, gets to his feet 'with a ponderous impetuosity, as a startled ox might scramble up from the grass' (p. 148), while punctiliously declaring his inability to contemplate the worth of existence when honour has been lost, he shows himself in speech and deportment to be one of Marlow's benighted who 'go through life with eyes half shut, with dull ears, with dormant thoughts' (p. 143), and is remembered by him as having spoken his verdict 'in the passionless and definite phraseology a machine would use, if machines could speak' (p. 159). Marlow is discomposed by the man's relentless rectitude, but his representation of the encounter acts to alienate affection from this impeccable practitioner of the tradition of the sea, by his making space for a sympathetic hearing to the cause he is pleading on behalf of one who has profaned that custom.[6]

The last antagonist to Marlow's heretical commitment, and the one who musters the most sophisticated arguments, is the only member of his original audience who was later and by letter 'privileged' to learn about the outcome of events concerning Jim, a man wholly devoted to those doctrines underpinning imperialism which on Marlow's expanded horizon are now visible as epistemologically unsound and morally suspect. Without dissenting from the dogmas of his correspondent on the necessity for colonial actions to be based 'on a firm conviction in the truth of ideas racially our own, in whose name are established the order, the morality, of an ethical progress' (p. 339), or for colonialism's servants to fight in the ranks if their lives are to count – indeed by dissembling with the disclaimer, 'I affirm nothing' – Marlow vindicates the integrity of one who had defected from the mission and yet remained faithful to principles, and whose subsequent gallantry intimates his confessing 'to a faith mightier than the laws of order and progress' (p. 339). Just as Marlow is an active agent in Jim's fate, so does the relationship with Jim destroy his confidence in the platitudes solemnly spoken by the unnamed 'privileged' man, and it is with some bitterness that he reflects on the smallness of his own achievement in having kept his place in

the ranks of an insignificant multitude. Where Marlow's interlocutors regard the rules governing their particular social order as
objectively validated and permanently valid moral imperatives,
he, because of responding to the imponderables in Jim's situation,
is disturbed by 'the most obstinate ghost of man's creation . . . the
doubt of the sovereign power enthroned in a fixed standard of
conduct' (p. 50), misgivings which, in one who had sought to rely
on the moral guidance provided by a guild, signify a critical
juncture in his construction of an alternative ethic. His sardonic
estimate of Jim's pious father, who is convinced that the existing
system is the best of all possible worlds and regards the social
utilities of his inequitable society as ethical axioms, has the
authority of the lapsed believer looking back on those few simple
notions he had once trusted as adequate to direct and sustain a
worthy existence, and coming to terms with the need to discover
or devise an ultimate authority for morality commensurate with
dynamic historical circumstances and variously orientated value
systems: 'The old chap goes on equably trusting Providence and
the established order of the universe . . . Virtue is one all over the
world, and there is only one faith, one conceivable conduct of life,
one manner of dying' (p. 341).

Because for Marlow the real significance of crime is that it
breaks faith with the community of mankind, he cannot but admit
that Jim in deserting his fellows stands accused of more than
professional misconduct. Yet without abandoning this definition,
he seeks for wholly other standards by which Jim's self-evident
flaws and obvious qualities can be measured, and he finds these in
an aspiration outside and hostile to the authorised commandments of imperialist society – in the pursuit of visionary desires
that unfit the dreamer for fulfilling socially appointed functions
which serve to perpetuate the existing order. Having instinctively
condemned Jim as a traitor to his calling, Marlow, in response to
a feeling wider than the fellowship of the craft, forges a bond of
intimacy with the apostate, and while he characteristically
deprecates the emotion as egoism, what he demonstrates in his
concern for the living Jim and his epitaph to a dead comrade is a
disinterested love for a friend or a child that survives, and is
strengthened by, the detestation of the conformist and the
obloquy of those who guard the established order of society. But
Marlow does more, and where the first narrator automatically
expels Jim from the community of his own kind, he examines the

roots to moral precepts and the ethical foundations to socially
ordained action in an effort to prove that despite his culpability,
Jim remains 'one of us'.

It has so far been argued that the discourse in *Lord Jim* produces a
critique of imperialism's official ethos; all the same there are
compelling reasons for reading it as a novel that manifestly has
not cut the umbilical cord connecting it with the dominant
ideology. In the *Author's Note* appended almost two decades after
the work was published, Conrad wrote that on conceiving the
person of Jim, it had been his wish 'with all the sympathy of which
I was capable, to seek fit words for his meaning. He was "one of
us" ' (p. ix). The generality of this last phrase leaves it open to a
number of constructions, and common to the possible interpretations which the text can support is the notion of a closed and elect
group (the club, the regiment, the religious order, the guild, the
masonic lodge), a concept critically different in sentiment from
the ecumenical embrace signified in the quotation used as the
Epigraph to *Youth: A Narrative and Two Other Stories*, the volume
which includes *Heart of Darkness*, and that could as appropriately
be inscribed on the tombstone of the Marlow met with in *Lord Jim*:
'. . . But the dwarf answered: "No; something human is dearer to
me than the wealth of all the world" '. Because Conrad in his
retrospective preface is addressing a readership deemed capable
of identifying the unspecified aggregate, just as Marlow tells his
tale to cronies connected with colonial trade who would share an
idiom and whom he includes as belonging within the undefined
fraternity, it is easy to suppose that the incantatory refrain to
which Marlow time and again returns implies Jim's membership
of the merchant navy and more broadly, the British Service
Classes. Certainly when first assessing Jim's person and milieu,
Marlow salutes that company from which the Empire recruited
its servants as an aristocracy of the trustworthy and the valiant:
'He stood there for all the parentage of his kind, for men and
women by no means clever or amusing, but whose very existence is
based upon honest faith, and upon the instinct of courage' (p. 43).
But as Marlow does not see himself as belonging with 'that
good, stupid kind we like to feel marching right and left of us in
life, of the kind that is not disturbed by the vagaries of intelligence
and the perversions of – of nerves, let us say' (p. 44), and is in
rebellion against those who have immunised themselves against

'the intensity of life' and blinded themselves to new ways of seeing, it would seem that the identity of this society needs to be sought elsewhere; and in a fiction which discovers the ultimate sanctions for moral consciousness to reside in the indwelling essence of the nation and the race, the words 'one of us' can be seen to take on a more portentous and precise ideological meaning. If by using the phrase 'community of mankind' Marlow infers the existence of one international and indivisible human collective, then the universality of this concept is countermanded by his paean to a Homeland perceived as the guardian spirit giving guidance and shelter only to its own:

I was going home – to that home distant enough for all its hearthstones to be like one hearthstone, by which the humblest of us has the right to sit. We wander in our thousands over the face of the earth, the illustrious and the obscure, earning beyond the seas our fame, our money, or only a crust of bread; but it seems to me that for each of us going home must be like going to render an account. We return to face our superiors, our kindred, our friends – those whom we obey, and those whom we love; but even they who have neither, the most free, lonely, irresponsible and bereft of ties, – even those for whom home holds no dear face, no familiar voice, – even they have to meet the spirit that dwells within the land, under its sky, in its air, in its valleys, and on its rises, in its fields, in its waters and its trees – a mute friend, judge, and inspirer . . . But the fact remains that you must touch your reward with clean hands, lest it turn to dead leaves, to thorns, in your grasp. I think it is the lonely, without a fireside or an affection they may call their own, those who return not to a dwelling but to the land itself, to meet its disembodied, eternal, and unchangeable spirit – it is those who understand best its severity, its saving power, the grace of its secular right to our fidelity, to our obedience. Yes! few of us understand, but we all feel it though, and I say *all* without exception, because those who do not feel do not count. Each blade of grass has its spot on earth whence it draws its life, its strength; and so is man rooted to the land from which he draws his faith together with his life. I don't know how much Jim understood; but I know he felt, he felt confusedly but power-fully, the demand of some such truth or some such illusion. (pp. 221–2)

To read in this eulogy the yearnings of an author who had known the deracination of exile is a necessary but insufficient observation, for while it does describe the emotions that inform the passage, it avoids engaging with the function of the speech within the text, which is to designate the nature of the compact uniting a moral community, and as a consequence, to establish that in this commonwealth Jim, who had forfeited his mariner's licence, had not lost his place.

Because the fiction's argument can find no final authority attesting to the truth of fixed and invariable standards, and concludes that the official ethic is determined by utilitarian imperatives and institutional needs, the historical determinants of moral concepts are established, and it becomes necessary to seek for the source and arbiter of exemplary conduct outside the confines of the pragmatic rules governing any particular and mortal social order, and beyond the bewildering plurality of diverse faiths and incommensurable value systems. With his nostalgia for stable and integrated social formations where there had existed both an identity of public role and individual desire and a coherence of moral thinking, and which he knew had been shattered by historical changes in the West, Conrad in *Lord Jim* recovers the idea of a moral consensus and locates this as immanent in the idea of the eternal nation, where a continuing tradition embodied in unchanging mores commanding fidelity to agreed purposes is binding on all classes and through the ages. It is loyalty to such an unwritten, uncodified and ahistorical ethos that the fiction proffers as the valid basis of solidarity, and since Jim never ceases to pay homage to the precepts of this common-wealth – 'The thing is that in virtue of his feeling he mattered' (p. 222) – he remains by that definition and by Marlow's valuation, 'one of us'. A conscience mirroring the 'soul' of his homeland and a consciousness of having broken faith with a due obligation to serve its will admit Jim to a universe from which a specified group of the fiction's other wanderers are forever exiled – the skipper, mate and engineer of the *Patna* who deserted the ship out of cowardice and then justified their flight, the degenerate mariners frequenting the eastern seaports, seduced and enslaved by a life of ease, the lawless latter-day buccaneers hungry for excitement and gain, the depraved Chester and Robinson obsessed with a scheme for wrenching wealth from a waterless guano island. In the context of Marlow's deference for the tutelage provided by home, it becomes apparent that the function of these peripheral characters, all of whom are connected with colonial service, trade or adventure, is to display that they violate the moral consensus of their cultural community by traducing the spiritually inspired colonial impulse. With the violent intrusion of Gentleman Brown as the fiction's archetypal antagonist to all morality and the mythic perverter of imperialism's positive intent, the boundaries of the moral republic are delineated to incorporate those whose unwavering allegiance is to the dominant aspiration of the nation, and this in the world of the novel is incarnate as imperialism. Thus a reading of Marlow's key speech, one which is spoken in the voice of the exiled colonial servant and addressed to an immediate audience who are participants in the same experience, will reveal the presence of our old friend the redeeming idea and will show that what Marlow is concerned to prove is how Jim's fidelity to imperialism's saving ideals establishes him, despite his defection, as 'one of us'.

That variable meanings can be constructed from Marlow's peroration on home and his repeated use of the phrase 'one of us', points up the text's equivocal relationship with received ideas, for on its simplest level his words can legitimately be construed as a patriotic eulogy and an affirmation of ethnic solidarity delivered without irony by a protagonist possessed of a rich sardonic vein, and who on other occasions derides the ignorance of chauvinism and the arrogance of racism. Such an interpretation of Marlow's meaning, and one which shows him as an ally of the 'privileged' man, suggests that the elusive community is none other than those who serve imperialism's cause in foreign parts, a proposition given credence by Marlow's view of Jim amongst the people of Patusan as 'a creature not only of another kind but of another essence' (p. 229), existing in 'total and utter isolation' from 'them'. This representation suggests the possibility of 'one of us' being a term of racial identification distinguishing the colonialists from the alien world of the other.[7] Marlow's most powerful impression is of Jim's dissociation from his foreign environment, and despite his elegaic recall of him 'dominating and yet in complete accord with his surroundings – with the life in the forests and with the life of men' (p. 175), it is only by placing him mentally in his father's rectory and amidst his serene and unconscious family where he stands out as an incongruous presence, that he can at last see him whole, 'returned at last, no longer a mere white speck at the heart of an immense mystery, but of full stature, standing disregarded amongst their untroubled shapes' (p. 342). In fashioning this image, Marlow communicates a belief in inalienable racial roots which forever fix even the alienated in the soil of their native culture, and it is this concept that he articulates in emphasising Jim's dubious relationship with Patusan: 'all his conquests, the trust, the fame, the friendships, the love – all these things that made him master had made him a captive, too . . . Jim the leader was a captive in every sense . . . Every day added a link to the fetters of that strange freedom . . . he was imprisoned within the very freedom of his power' (pp. 247, 262, 283). The contrast between the passionate asseveration of home as mute friend, judge and inspiration, and the regretful depreciation of Jim's enslavement to Patusan, cuts across the commendation of Jim's achievement and acts to foreground the fundamental flaw in the position of white rajahs.

Here Marlow enacts a dual function as iconographer and iconoclast of the colonial myth; by hailing Jim's triumph in bringing peace and prosperity to Patusan as evidence of the white man's energy, enterprise and ingenuity, he represents Jim as heir to the tradition of colonial chivalry; and in emphasising Jim's cultural autonomy and his estrangement from the foreign society that has given him his 'chance', Marlow denies himself the possibility of commemorating the legend. For he shows that it is not from his Malayan comrades and vassals that Jim seeks confirmation of his redemption, but from his peers back home, addressing his pledge of fealty to their codes and their ideals. So committed is the fiction to the power of patriotism and the sustenance afforded by the sense of national identity, that endorsement is given by an unexpected source; even Stein in whom the fiction sketches a portrait of a proto-internationalist, and whose preoccupation is with formulating the nature of the human vocation binding on the species rather than with the origins of the moral consensus uniting a community, appears to suffer a sense of territorial banishment. Having found refuge and fortune in the East, he bequeathes his renowned collection of beetles and butterflies to the small German town of his birth, 'Something of me. The best' (p. 205), a sentiment that echoes the yearnings of Jim sick for a home that he will not again see: 'I shall be faithful . . . I shall be faithful . . . Tell them . . .' (pp. 334, 335). Such uncontradicted articulations of devotion to the nation and the race which is insensible to the ethical values cherished by either, draws *Lord Jim* back into the orbit of traditional imperialist ideology from which the fiction's discourse on matters moral and metaphysical struggles to escape.

Impinging on the foregrounded ethical argument about the foundations of moral principles and the sanctions for principled conduct, is the surrounding and elliptical philosophical discussion which considers the mainspring and ends of action and resituates problems of social value within the larger conceptual context of a human telos. With the opening out of this discourse, the proposition maintained by the overt narrative voices in *The Nigger of the 'Narcissus'* that the good of any practice is inherent in the activity itself and derives from the successful completion of any given task is overtaken by a view discriminating between forms of performance and assigning worth only to those acts motivated by ideals and striving after the realisation of distant, millennial goals. Standing outside the utilitarian tradition fostered by imperialist civilisation is the posture represented by Stein, who enters the fiction as the *deus ex machina* in Jim's fate and stays to fulfil a yet more portentous function as the prophet of utopian aspiration, for it is his testament that rescues the claims of imagination and visionary anticipation from the contumely of ideologues teaching the necessity of a safe positivism. But even before and after Stein's distinctive accents are heard, there are in the text premonitions and echoes of his articulate refusal to accede to the repression of desire and the banishment of the dream. Marlow himself speaks out eloquently for the validity and nobility of ruling passions when he chastises the sober and successful men of affairs listening to his tale for having starved their imaginations to feed their bodies, and applauds the 'bizarre obstinacy of that desire' more powerful than greed which had induced the seventeenth-century traders to defy unknown seas and death in their zeal for pepper: 'To us, their less tried successors, they appear magnified, not as agents of trade but as instruments of a recorded destiny, pushing out into the unknown in obedience to an inward voice, to an impulse beating in the blood, to a dream of the future' (p. 227).

He is joined in his avowal of ontological expectation by the first narrator who, although initially scornful of Jim's hunger for the unattainable, recounts with sympathy the dissatisfactions haunt-

ing the 'privileged' man now retired to the comfort and security of
a London flat: 'No more horizons as boundless as hope, no more
twilights within the forests as solemn as temples, in the hot quest
of the Ever-undiscovered Country over the hill, across the stream,
beyond the wave' (p. 338). Both Marlow and the primary
narrator speak in praise of the ardour impelling the colonial
adventurers of old to heroic feats, but their acclaim is animated by
their honouring the liberating effect of the inspiration rather than
the immediate objects of their desire, and the ventures themselves
serve as metaphors of the pursuit of the future, and not as
instances of illustrious colonial achievement. However, it would
be alien to the fiction's dialectic if the doctrine of hope were to be
uncontradicted, and the passionate advocacy of utopian desire as
a spiritual necessity is moderated by the doubts that are made to
accrete around the person and teachings of Stein and, more
dangerously, by the negative form of the visionary impulse
incarnate in Gentleman Brown's rage to initiate the apocalypse.
Although Stein is introduced by Marlow as wise, trustworthy and
humane, a man of both physical courage and intrepid spirit, the
substance of his theories as well as the manner of his address
arouse Marlow's suspicions, an uneasiness that he communicates
in a constellation of allusions to Stein as a shade, a ghost gliding
through a twilight world, 'a shadow prowling amongst the graves
of butterflies' (p. 214), occupying an uninhabited and uninhabit-
able house, 'a crystalline void', silent as a crypt, with dark, empty
rooms, dead exhibits and an atmosphere of catacombs. But if
these mortuary images undermine Stein's standing as a guru able
to guide the living through the perplexities of the concrete world,
then what he has to say does all the same have authority as a
statement of a dissident ontological outlook, and even though his
gnomic utterances seem impossible of semantic explication, the
spirit rather than the letter of his words does issue as a coherent
declaration of faith in hope as the means of realising the human
vocation, and the creation of an alternative world as its authentic
end.

Ian Watt accounts for the contradictions in Stein's parable by
pointing out that the sentence, 'A man that is born falls into a
dream like a man who falls into the sea', had originally read 'A
man that is born is like a man who falls into the sea'.[8] Yet it could
be argued that the final wording, despite its greater opacity,
expresses more exactly the import of Stein's belief that in the face

of this generic dilemma, the human purpose is achieved through the exercise of imagination, the capacity for abstract thought, the ability to construct mental images, the urge to envisage the shape of the future, powers which distinguish the species from the magnificent butterfly that 'finds a little heap of dirt and sits still on it' (p. 213). It is Watt's contention that the main reason why Stein's parable resists any consensus of analysis is 'the patent asymmetry of its basic metaphor: there is nothing that can stand as a satisfactory opposite to the sea, and thus give some measure of concreteness both to the individual's struggle in the water, and to its different outcomes. This has been the main stumbling-block in most interpretations of "in the destructive element immerse" ' (op. cit., pp. 327–8). But such an antithesis does exist and is a focus for the fiction's representation of the dream as the source of ontologically significant action, since Stein's use of the swimmer-sea metaphor to communicate dynamic human will recurs in Marlow's trope of the sea as 'the very image of struggling mankind . . . with its labouring waves for ever rising, sinking, and vanishing to rise again' (p. 243), and this last has as its contrary 'the immovable forests rooted deep in the soil, soaring towards the sunshine, everlasting in the shadowy might of their tradition, like life itself' (p. 243). When Stein completes his self-interrupted exhortation with the words, 'In the destructive element immerse . . . That was the way. To follow the dream, and again to follow the dream – and so – *ewig – usque ad finem* . . .' (p. 214–15), the metaphors of sea and dream, travail and visionary longing come together to signify his belief in the arduous and continuous pursuit of the ideal; and ultimately it is this stance which the fiction develops as the true expression of the species' destiny, for the creed teaching passive deference to time-honoured custom, that is immanent in the primal landscape of unreconstructed nature, is disclaimed as a negation of the human essence.

Stein, who is the heir to German romanticism and a European tradition of political idealism that had led him to participate in the 1848 Revolution and forced him into exile after its defeat, is shown to be a paradigm of the effective romantic who had translated his aspirations into reality, dissolving in his own history as youthful radical and later as honourable adventurer and confidant of native rulers in the East, the artificial dichotomy between imagination and performance. Significantly, when he prepares to give Marlow his answer to the question he has framed as 'how to be', he uses the past tense – 'That was the way' – by this alluding to his own abandonment of a practice that he continues to enjoin on others, since he had in old age capitulated to the division between the prose and the poetry, mechanically overseeing his extensive commercial empire while deriving spiritual fulfilment from the lonely study of lepidoptera. Stein's pronouncements should therefore be read as a declaration of commitment to an idea spoken by one who, although personally disillusioned, continues to affirm the urge to envision and implement a transfigured human order. Thus even as he is in full verbal flight his speech is arrested, as if his inspiration had been destroyed by his move from the distant shadows of his dark room into the circle lit by the lamp, from the obscurity where fancy is bred, to the brightness where empirical fact is evident as the only truth. For Marlow this transition from confident delivery to murmured hesitancy appears as proof of his having no answers, or worse, that his advice is fraught with dangers:

> The whisper of his conviction seemed to open before me a vast and uncertain expanse, as of a crepuscular horizon on a plain at dawn – or was it, perchance, at the coming of the night? One had not the courage to decide; but it was a charming and deceptive light, throwing the impalpable poesy of its dimness over pitfalls – over graves. His life had begun in sacrifice, in enthusiasm for generous ideas; he had travelled very far, on various ways, on strange paths, and whatever he followed it had been without faltering, and therefore without shame and without regret. In so far he was right. That was the way, no doubt. Yet for all that the great plain on which men wander amongst graves and pitfalls remained very desolate under the impalpable poesy of its crepuscular light, overshadowed in the centre, circled with a bright edge as if surrounded by an abyss full of flames. (p. 215)

Marlow's dissatisfaction with Stein's philosophy rests on its avoidance of practical difficulties, its romantic embrace of the hazards and failures associated with quixotic ventures; all the same the images in which he couches his mistrust communicate contradictory signals, some discrediting Stein's solutions as perilous and incapable of consummation, and others acknowledging that acolytes of utopianism must and will endure risk and defeat in pursuit of transcendent goals.

Thus although doubt does attach to Stein's prescriptions, his posture is not repudiated by the fiction and is even given oblique validation in Marlow's elegy to Jim, which offers in his death a triumph denied to Brierly's demoralised suicide, for this lament is irradiated by esteem for Jim's sacrifice to the dream, his fidelity to a shadowy ideal of conduct, his surrender to the claim of his own world of shades. Because Jim's passion is mediated by Marlow, who against the grain of his creed acts as a witness for ideas that are not his own, the 'impossible world of romantic achievement' (p. 83), whose realisation must be deferred to a future time, survives in the text as an emblem of the will to initiate a transfigured tomorrow. Yet because the fiction's discourse generates its own antithesis, an opposite form of the utopian inspiration manifests itself, one that is also motivated by a refusal of the here and now, and in Gentleman Brown, 'a blind accomplice of the Dark Powers' (p. 354), an archetypal figure of the non-rational will that pits itself against the established order and defies history, exults in destruction and looks on the world as its prey, the fiction produces the enemy of hope and the architect of cosmic cataclysm:

> There was in the broken, violent speech of that man, unveiling before me his thoughts with the very hand of Death upon his throat, an undisguised ruthlessness of purpose, a strange vengeful attitude towards his own past, and a blind belief in the righteousness of his will against all mankind, something of that feeling which could induce the leader of a horde of cut-throats to call himself proudly the Scourge of God. (p. 370)

It is this embodiment of the exterminating angel, a being 'moved by some complex intention' (p. 353) in his ambition to strew the earth with corpses and envelop it in flames, who stands as a warning of the dangers to the messianic imagination and serves to redefine the contours of a positive millenarianism.

In a fiction that is disillusioned in a creed of action from which the question of goals beyond immediate necessity is expunged, and converted to the conception of activity as a means to the realisation of ideal ends, the dialogue is between incommensurable western ideologies and the introduction of a foreign code negating the principle of performance and orientated towards

Nirvana engenders no power to challenge the terms of the discussion. If the quest for repose and the annihilation of desire which lies at the heart of eastern metaphysics and is peripheral to all religious systems is allowed a voice, it is repudiated as a denial of the ultimate human ends projected by the fiction. Marlow's tolerance towards episodic lapses into the longing for peace is inseparable from his conviction that it signifies an abandonment of hope and with it abdication from the human vocation: 'Which of us here has not observed this, or maybe experienced something of that feeling in his own person – this extreme weariness of emotions, the vanity of effort, the yearning for rest?' (p. 88). The dream in its negative form as narcosis is embodied in the representation of Patusan, and if it does exist in the fiction as a highly articulated form of hierarchical and ritualised social existence, it is primarily a metaphysical landscape whose every feature departs from western conceptions of form, norm and value: 'do you notice how, three hundred miles beyond the end of telegraph cables and mail-boat lines, the haggard utilitarian lies of our civilisation wither and die, to be replaced by pure exercises of imagination, that have the futility, often the charm, and sometimes the deep hidden truthfulness of works of art?' (p. 282).

While Marlow's disenchantment with pragmatism does cause him to look with favour on a place still uncorrupted by technology, and through a balancing of antinomies to augur a validation of its immanent meanings, the ultimate vision of Patusan is realised in a configuration of negatives: it is timeless, immobile, a land without a past, one of the earth's lost, forgotten places, where the smells are primeval, the air stagnant and the old trees and old mankind exist in their original dusk of being:

A brooding gloom lay over this vast and monotonous landscape; the light fell on it as if into an abyss. The land devoured the sunshine . . . It remains in the memory motionless, unfaded, with its life arrested, in an unchanging light . . . I had turned away from the picture and was going back to a world where events move, men change, light flickers, life flows in a clear stream, no matter whether over mud or over stones . . . I breathed deeply, I revelled in the vastness of the opened horizons, in the different atmosphere that seemed to vibrate with a toil of life, with the energy of an impeccable world. (pp. 264, 330, 331)

In communicating his hostile perceptions of an alien and estranging world and confirming the worth of his own culture, Marlow returns to the conventional connotations of the dark and invokes the established dichotomy between the error of inertia and the good of action, for whereas to him the people of Patusan appear to exist 'as if under an enchanter's wand', Jim 'lives', a contrast between passivity and volition that signifies respectively human purpose denied and enacted; and while he recoils from the pristine and featureless vistas of the unreconstructed East, he takes delight in Stein's artificial gardens where the local vegetation had been brought together in a fluted grove of exquisite beauty and grace. With this the fiction invites its audience to applaud initiative, creative imagination and the will to transform the environment as victories against the stasis of repetitive custom, unvarying habit and immemorial usage, and since the contrast is embodied in the polarised structures of West and East, the West is rescued from the onslaught made by the text on its contemporary ambitions and terms of seeing.

But if no salvation is discovered in the rival goals of another civilisation and the text produces eccentric versions of dominant conceptual categories, *Lord Jim* does dramatise a radical critique of imperialist ideology that is directed against a spiritually repressive culture demanding unreflective obedience to the laws of order and progress, misrepresenting social utilities in the service of class interests as moral axioms and restricting the definition of knowledge to exclude meditations on alternative human conditions. Yet the novel itself begets no prefigurations of the content to the dreams of the future, nor how these are to be given corporeal form, and this absence can be adduced to the discontinuity between the significations of past historical circumstances which is the subject of the narrative, and a political and theological critique of a contemporary ethos, between the regretful demystification of the legend about colonial romance, and the determined censure of the utilitarian philosophy inspiring the imperialism of a later epoch. Because the fiction locates the manifestations of idealistic intent and significant action in the past, and interprets this bygone age as if the succeeding era were not already visible and the future therefore still unknowable, the death of Jim and the frustration of his hopes necessarily leaves the political horizon empty, for the consummation of promise cannot be represented by a triumphant imperialism that has been

Conrad and Imperialism

disavowed by the text. Thus in a novel which rescues victory from a tale of total defeat, the fiction's vatic impulses are constrained to issue as illuminations of the human need to anticipate and possess the future, but without intimations of who the architects of the new age will be or what it is they are striving to construct.

6 *Nostromo*

It may seem self-evident that *Nostromo* is a hermeneutical chronicle of a society in transition from old colonialism to new imperialism. But since the novel is a meditation on the meaning of history and produces a perspective on historical narrative which moves between the poles of the political and the theological, joining social critique of a particular condition with abstract moral testament, the function of history within its polysemous registers has elicited diverse and incompatible analyses. For those critics whose readings map the fiction's moral, metaphysical, psychological or mythic worlds as a space where the archetypal individual grapples with universal destiny, history is peripheral to what is seen as an essentially existential struggle. An altogether different critical approach also relegating history is used by Edward Said in an interpretation which engages with the fiction's foregrounded public dimensions in order to locate its significance elsewhere. What Said proposes is that since the real action underlying the political and historical events in *Nostromo* is psychological and concerns man's overambitious intention to author his own world because the world as he finds it is somehow intolerable, the subjective personality of the work criticises and undermines the objective structure, making of it 'a novel about political history that is reduced, over the course of several hundred pages, to a condition of mind, an inner state'.[1]

Even within the practice of political criticism there are differences in interpreting what kind of history *Nostromo* writes, the ways history is inscribed in the text and how this is to be made known by critical discussion. Irving Howe claims that the novel may be read as 'a fictional study of imperialism' that presents 'a coherent social world . . . in which all the relevant political tendencies are finely balanced, one against the other' (op. cit., pp. 100, 101); for Eloise Knapp Hay (op. cit.) it is a political novel where historical processes are offered as the real subject of the story; Avrom Fleishman maintains that: 'The novel marks the fulfilment of Conrad's political imagination: it represents the history of a society as a living organism. Indeed the complex narrative structure of the novel reflects this sense of history's unfolding processes' (op. cit., p. 161); and Gareth Jenkins, who examines the ideological tensions hidden within the work's 'curious chronological distortions and narrative complexities', finds that the book not only reflects history but incorporates 'a sustained commentary through its formal narrative structure on its own action' which is calculated to deny the possibility of real change and expose history as illusory (op. cit., p. 138). In a virtuoso ' "metacommentary", or the historical and dialectical reevaluation of conflicting interpretative methods', Fredric Jameson, who argues that literary texts should be seen as socially symbolic acts, an approach which replaces the mechanistic notion of text and context with concepts of production, compensation, repression and displacement as forms of the dynamic relationship existing between empirical text and the prior historical or ideological subtext, demonstrates how the social and political content is repressed beneath the surface of the fiction's formal structures:

> *Nostromo* is thus ultimately, if you like, no longer a political or historical novel, no longer a realistic representation of history; yet in the very movement in which it represses such content and seeks to demonstrate the impossibility of such representation, by a wondrous dialectical transfer the historical 'object' itself becomes inscribed in the very form. (*The Political Unconscious*, p. 280)

For critics who are constrained by choice of method or methodological limitations to confine discussion to the procedures through which the canonical text reveals and criticises dominant ideological forms, the attempt to construct *Nostromo*'s meanings within political parameters will come up against those countervailing tendencies contained by the fiction's multivalent discourse and which coalesce to deny that events can be conceptually constituted as 'history'. Thus analysis of the dynamics to manifest processes contends with speculation on history as contingency, the dramatisation of social conflict is in competition with the re-enactment of myth, the language of political discussion is rivalled by a form of address appropriate to revelation and prophecy, and protagonists who are representative figures of specific social practices and cultural traditions and are known by a title denoting an occupation, a status or a cause – the Capataz de Cargadores, the engineer-in-chief, the First Lady of Sulaco, the Garibaldino – are simultaneously conceived as stylised embodiments of generic qualities or flaws and could be named Vanity, Service, Compassion and Principle. It can therefore be said that the coherence of historical narrative is demonstrated and repudiated, and a criticism of imperialism's ideology which looks to its social matrix is undercut by a moral fable where the imperialist inspiration figures as the most recent incarnation of original sin and permanent folly. This movement between materialist and metaphysical perceptions itself constitutes an epistemological dialogue on how phenomena and movements existing in time are to be apprehended. So paradigmatic is Conrad's Costaguana, its official name and informal designation as the Treasure House of the World, like those of the Gold Coast, the Ivory Coast and the Argentine marks of the conspicuous objects of colonialist desire, its primeval landscape, turbulent politics and trajectory from stagnant traditionalism to anarchic decadence meeting the expectations of an audience casually acquainted with western-centric accounts of Latin America's violent history and degenerate collective character, that readers both then and now could mistake this most ideological of configurations for an authentic transmutation of an 'objective' reality.[2] But the function of a 'realism' which is itself culturally perceived and politically tendentious, is to predetermine the scenario of the war between the hemispheres where a historical view on the invasion of other worlds by imperialism is interpenetrated by a transhistorical perspective of the contest between Reason and Passion, Ego and Id, the Principles of Performance and Pleasure.

Yet it will be argued that as narrated by *Nostromo*, the convulsive transformation of a Latin American republic from the reign of arbitrary oppression imposed by indigenous oligarchs and populist dictators to the structured exploitation organised by international finance capitalism, is an exercise in historical interpretation which departs from authorised accounts, for the book's vision is of changes in economic and social conditions generating alterations in consciousness, and of hostile class forces locked in struggle. Whereas in *Heart of Darkness* and *Lord Jim* the central figures are represented as individual products and victims of historical circumstances, pressing against the frontiers of their given situation and destroyed by their presumption, 'history' as the collective project of human agents is itself the principal protagonist in *Nostromo* and the destiny of an entire social order its subject. Here no mediating voices soliciting the readers' complicity in this stance or that intercede between the text and its reception since all communication is controlled by an omniscient narrator overseeing the movement of dispersed aspects to converging events, delivering a commentary where disparate possibilities of interpretation are mooted, discounted or endorsed, and interpolating *ex cathedra* pronouncements on the action which do not constitute a consistent outlook. Where in the other fictions the interlocution of centres of intelligence illuminates and criticises conventional categories of thought, and when he is present Marlow records his own passage from trust in the norms and values of his culture to a radical agnosticism, in *Nostromo* it is the disjunction between the text's immanent meanings and the narrative assertions, condemnations and celebrations which reveal viewpoints at odds with the persuasion declared or inferred by the narrator, and that makes this a radical political fiction mediated by a deeply conservative consciousness.

Conrad was careful to point out that Nostromo was not the hero of the Tale of the Seaboard but, by giving the familiar name of this protagonist to the book, he found a totalising trope signifying essential themes in the fiction's myriad political and ethical discussions. For the title, with its multiple and dissonant resonances denoting and superseding an array of literal meanings, has more comprehensive and variegated sets of referents than those accreting about the eponymous figure and which reach to the heart of the novel's critique of a civilisation founded on the sanctity of property. To the English of Sulaco, Giovanni Battista Fidanza is known as 'Nostromo', the Italian for boatswain[3] and therefore an apt nickname for the Italian foreman of compatriot and Basque dockers who alternatively refer to him as the Capataz de Cargadores. However, because Nostromo is a designation despised and rejected by the holder's surrogate Italian family as one bestowed by the English masters, and that is properly no word at all, this points towards other intended meanings, and confirms suggestions that it is a corruption of *nostro uoma*, our man.

The title therefore functions as a metonym for an ethos that, by consecrating the private ownership of property, legitimises the concept of the person as a possession:[4] Captain Mitchell, the author of the mispronunciation, innocently boasts of Nostromo as 'my capataz', 'that fellow of mine', a chattel whom he enthusiastically lends to the other Europeans of Sulaco; the officials of the British-owned Railway Company look on the President-Dictator of the Republic, brought to power through the support of the Blanco aristocrats and the backing of the foreign investors, as 'their own creature' (p. 38), and the American millionaire Holroyd exults in his connection with the Gould Mining Concession because: 'He was not running a great enterprise there; no mere railway board or industrial corporation. He was running a man!' (p. 81). Nor do these connotations exhaust the immanent meanings of the word, and the text develops a different set of associations that counterbalance the implications of servitude with those of autonomy. On the one hand Nostromo is conceived and exists not only as the functionary of his class enemies, but as a man *of* the people, *their* Great Man, an identity implying another sense of affiliation that is stressed in Conrad's *Preface* (pp. xiii, xv) and affirmed by the protagonist who speaks of himself as 'a man of the people' (p. 301). On the other hand, Mitchell's invaluable subordinate, the lackey of the native oligarchs and the factotum of the Europeans, whose sense of personal worth is dependent on the good opinion of his overlords and the sycophancy of his underlings, shows himself to be above all else, his own person: 'It concerns me to keep on being what I am: every day alike' (p. 253).

The perspective on the rights of ownership as a dubious ethos opens the way to a larger discussion on the tenets and goals that had come to dominate western thinking, and whereas in the global cultural contest registered by the fiction the West features as the human norm righteously battling against deviations, in the moral drama where Latin America plays no part, that civilisation which had gained possession of the whole world and lost its own soul is cast in the role of a fallen state. The conflict between the advancement of secular concerns and the defence of spiritual values is posed in terms appropriate to a religious discourse, and the counterposing of utilitarian exigencies to moral ideas as articulated by Dr Monygham ['There is no peace and no rest in the development of material interests. They have their law, and their justice. But it is founded on expediency, and is inhuman; it is without rectitude, without the continuity and the force that can be found only in a moral principle' (p. 511)] and echoed by Emilia

Gould ['There was something inherent in the necessities of successful action which carried with it the moral degradation of the idea' (p. 521)], registers a conception of two incommensurable realms which conforms to categories of western sacred thought.

In a text where notions of sin, transgression, redemption, the traffic in souls and transactions with the devil enter into the characters' self-analysis and occur as objective explanations of their conduct, the use of an iconography and essential symbolism which draws on scriptural sources brings a religious dimension to the terms of the ethical discourse: the sculptured likeness of Emilia Gould's purity and compassion is the Madonna in the niche of the Casa Gould; and the mines which dominate the action as an autonomous force are conceived in the awesome image of Moloch, its yield in the early days paid for 'in its own weight of human bones' (p. 52), now seen by Nostromo as hateful, immense and of unlimited power and by Mrs Gould as a fetish and a weight: 'More soulless than any tyrant, more pitiless and autocratic than the worst government; ready to crush innumerable lives in the expansion of its greatness' (p. 521). Echoes of biblical usage also accrete around the central symbol: as a substance of incorruptible physical properties and lustrous appearance, silver in western vocabulary is an equivalent of purity and the antiquated term for a silver coin still survives as a synonym for admirable qualities of character and standards of excellence. Yet the fiction's disavowal of a society's morality which derives from its worship of silver as an 'emblem of a common cause, the symbol of the supreme importance of material interests' (p. 260), evokes the admonitions delivered in Job's parable,[5] and the taint it carries as the currency paid for the primal act of treachery in the story of Christ is indwelling in its fictional incarnation. It is this that makes Nostromo's cry, 'I die betrayed – betrayed by – ', and the comment, 'but he did not say by whom and by what he was dying betrayed' (p. 559), a sardonic reference back to its perfidious role in Christian literature. Such allusions to the incompatibility of the sacred and the secular come together in the text's counterbalancing of fear and loathing for materialistic preoccupations and reverence for asceticism which reiterates an antinomy fundamental to New Testament teaching:

No man can serve two masters: for either he will hate the one,

and love the other; or else he will hold to one, and despise the
other. Ye cannot serve God and Mammon.
Therefore I say unto you, Be not anxious for your life, what ye
shall eat, or what ye shall drink; nor yet for your body, what ye
shall put on. Is not the life more than the food, and the body
than the raiment?
(Matthew 6: 24, 25)

In that *Nostromo* constructs a moral argument against fetishising
material objects and censures the cult of acquisitiveness, it
undercuts the ethical sanctions attached by the ideologues of
capitalist civilisation to the principle and institution of private
ownership, and in speculating on the hypothesis that property is
theft, the text generates its most subversive insight. If no moral
basis for the possession of wealth exists, then to steal from the rich
cannot be construed as a crime, and the bandit Hernandez, driven
off the land by the oppressions of landlords and corrupt government, is not conceived as a thief. This unorthodox perspective on
the rights of property enters the discussion of Nostromo's theft,
which is represented as both an act of defiance against an
institution and a parody of the process whereby the wealthy
acquire their riches, and that they would claim to be founded on
some prior natural law. Yet although Nostromo's accusation and
defence, 'The rich live on wealth stolen from the people' (p. 541) is
abundantly validated by the fiction's action and discourse, it
would be absurd to claim that this is a novel which takes the
momentous step of endorsing the commandment to expropriate
the expropriators, and the reiterated use of the epithets
'accursed', 'forbidden' and 'unlawful' in conjunction with treasure
only, implies that legitimate forms of property do exist and are
inviolable, and by inference, that theft is therefore both a felony
and a sin. At the very point where the text concedes that no ethical
sanction for the ownership of property can be found, it vitiates its
own argument by dramatising theft as a moral transgression. It is
this latter perspective that is developed by the fiction's fable about
the curse of stolen treasure in which Nostromo is destined to
re-enact the craving and the punishment of mythic adventurers
who had defied a prohibition on searching for the gold of
Costaguana's high mountains and had died with their souls tied
for eternity to their temptation: 'And the feeling of fearful and
ardent subjection, the feeling of his slavery – so irremediable and

profound that often, in his thoughts, he compared himself to the legendary Gringos, neither dead nor alive, bound down to their conquest of unlawful wealth on Azuera – weighed heavily on the independent Captain Fidanza' (pp. 526–7). With this the rebel who disdains a system based on the worship of property is displaced by the perpetrator, and victim, of a crime against property, and as the ground of the discussion moves from history to theology, so is the critique of private property obscured by denunciation of the power greed can exercise over human will and which afflicts the whole human race: 'There is no credulity so eager and blind as the credulity of covetousness, which, in its universal extent, measures the moral misery and the intellectual destitution of mankind' (p. 450).

A consequence of such strictures on enthralment to things material is that, in a story of spectacular worldly success, it is the unworldly protagonists who are exemplars of moral conduct. At the centre of this group of secular saints who share a gravity of soul, an austerity of disposition and disinterested devotion to noble ideals [these include Linda Viola, praised for her exacting standards of duty and faithfulness, the serene and serious Antonia Avellanos, modelled according to Conrad on his first love, 'an uncompromising Puritan of patriotism with no taint of the slightest worldliness in her thoughts' (*Preface*, p. xiv), Emilia Gould 'full of endurance and compassion' and uncorrupted by mercenary ambitions, and Dr Monygham whose every action is 'exalted by a spiritual detachment from the usual sanctions of hope and reward' (p. 431)], is Giorgio Viola, the old Garibaldino:

> The spirit of self-forgetfulness, the simple devotion to a vast humanitarian ideal which inspired the thought and stress of that revolutionary time, had left its mark upon Giorgio in a sort of austere contempt for all personal advantage. This man, whom the lowest classes in Sulaco suspected of having a buried hoard in his kitchen, had all his life despised money. The leaders of his youth had lived poor, had died poor. It had been a habit of his mind to disregard to-morrow ... It did not resemble the carelessness of a condottiere, it was a puritanism of conduct, born of stern enthusiasm like the puritanism of religion. (p. 31)

Such veneration of 'severe and immaculate' persons who choose self-denial and look upon devotion to a cause as a gift and not a sacrifice, sets the standard for assessing the motives of those other Puritans inspired by 'an insatiable imagination of conquest' (p. 76), driven by an appetite for self-righteousness and goaded by the hunger for self-aggrandisement.

To recognise that the tenets of western religious traditions are integral to the novel's ethical discourse, is not to categorise *Nostromo* as a religious fiction, and indeed veneration for the numinous is noticeable by its absence. Still it is a term with theological associations which is a key-word in the fiction's vocabulary and it is necessary to see how this approximates to the concept of belief in a being whose presence can neither be seen nor proven. As used in the book, faith excludes the aspiration to withdraw from the proper exercise of responsibility within the quotidian world and signifies rather a form of consciousness manifest in the performance of duties that serve collective needs and pursue corporate ends. The relationship in which faith is placed to action and intellect confirms that it is conceived as the basic principle in a social ethic and not as the apprehension of a divine presence; and in a novel which joins a narrative about initiative and deeds with speculation on the moral foundations to performance, action is depreciated as 'the enemy of thought and the friend of flattering illusions' (p. 66) feeding a false sense of mastery over the fates, and intelligence disclaimed as a snare impeding the development of spiritual resources. Just as Nostromo is said to be the 'victim of the disenchanted vanity which is the reward of audacious action', so is Decoud described as, 'A victim of the disillusioned weariness which is the retribution meted out to intellectual audacity' (p. 501), and to illustrate this perception the presence of books and weapons in Charles Gould's study points up an absence that is filled by the icon to which Emilia Gould pays obeisance.

In order to establish the authority of Faith, the text defames other experiential modes where belief in moral absolutes and devotion to social ideals is not binding, to this end interceding with an insistently hostile gloss calculated to traduce a luminous representation of Nothingness. Decoud's dislocation in the solitude of the Gulf's silent darkness is shown as that state where the ego merges 'into the world of cloud and water, of natural forces and forms of nature' and the universe appears as 'a succession of incomprehensible images' (p. 497):

In this foretaste of eternal peace they [his thoughts] floated
vivid and light, like unearthly clear dreams of earthly things
that may haunt the souls freed by death from the misty
atmosphere of regrets and hopes . . . All his active sensations
and feelings from as far back as he could remember seemed to
him the maddest of dreams . . . the stillness was so profound
that Decoud felt as if the slightest sound conceivable must
travel unchecked and audible to the end of the world. (pp. 262,
267, 284)

A consciousness of meaninglessness as the ultimate reality can be
known by believer and sceptic alike and under a different name is
the condition prized by mystics as the final beatitude and sought
by them when they remove themselves to caves, mountain tops,
the desert and deserted shores. But because Decoud is on trial for
cynicism and the error of recognising no other virtue than
intelligence, his knowledge of Nirvana and subsequent suicide are
interpreted as the inevitable consequences of his lack of convictions, principles and ideals. Thus the authenticity of an experience validated by different ontological theories must be denied
because it is a denial of Faith: 'The brilliant Costaguanero of the
boulevards had died from solitude and want of faith in himself and
others . . . The brilliant "Son Decoud", the spoiled darling of the
family, the lover of Antonia and journalist of Sulaco, was not fit to
grapple with himself single-handed' (pp. 496, 497).
    To compound the denigration of Decoud, the fatal faults in a
man whom Father Corbelàn scorns as a godless materialist are
weighed and judged against the virtues of Dr Monygham, who
had lost his honour by betraying his associates under torture but
retained belief in 'a rule of conduct resting mainly on severe
rejections' and 'had made himself an ideal conception of his
disgrace' (p. 375). This conception of faith as an ethical imperative determines the ways in which the claims of other philosophical outlooks are communicated, and just as the book's title
condenses a spectrum of related and disjunctive meanings
developed by the political discourse, so do the names of the
constituent parts which designate three locations vital to the
fiction's action serve as emblems of incompatible modes of
awareness and warring systems of value. 'The Silver of the Mine'
is both the visible product of technological achievement and the
'symbol of the supreme importance of material interests', and as

such represents both a positivist stance and the reified form of a society's values. In 'The Isabels', three uninhabited islands set down in a Gulf that is deaf, dumb, blind and which no intelligence can penetrate, the fiction transfigures an archaic universe, 'the whole scheme of things of which we form a helpless part . . . the immense indifference of things', and with this a response that pessimistically rejects the phenomenal world as a place without value. If the first can be seen as 'culture' and the second as 'nature', then 'The Lighthouse', built on the largest of the islands which before its coming had been shunned even by the birds, is a figure of visionary anticipation: with its lamps like 'some sacred flame' sending a yellow beam 'far above the shames and passion of the earth' and towards the 'far horizon', it signifies the urge to reach out to the always invisible future. Within this spectrum, the densely historical moment of the novel's action is inserted into a time-continuum spanning the measureless ages of a cosmos immensely old, and leaving open that space which is yet to be occupied by human history. It is this inclusive prospect connecting the present both to its known origins and to its indeterminate outcome, and looking on history as a continuous and continuing human narrative, that is seen by Emilia Gould in her despair at having placed the exigencies of immediate practical need before the aspiration to distant goals which respects tradition even while exceeding it: 'It had come into her mind that for life to be large and full, it must contain the care of the past and of the future in every passing moment of the present. Our daily work must be done to the glory of the dead and for the good of those who come after' (pp. 520–1). With this the conflict between faith and action is transcended by the introduction of a prospect where the two are joined in the utopian desire to realise an ideal world. Against the grain of a rhetoric deriding the efficacy of politics and vilifying the practices of radical movements, and in defiance of a perspective that disparages the visionary impulse of social hope as chimerical, the text engenders an opposite vision in which politics is seen as the agency of deliverance from the soulless materialism of a debased world.

To the extent that *Nostromo* is Conrad's most uncompromising criticism of the West's moral decline, it is also an ardent vindication of European values as a theoretical construct of surpassing excellence, and the polemical dimensions of the novel

can be seen to have fundamental affinities with the tract
'Autocracy and War' (1905),[6] written soon after the completion of
the book and inspired by the Japanese defeat of Russia in
Manchuria. This provided Conrad with a further occasion to
denounce Russia as the enemy of the western heritage, only here
castigation of Russian despotism and backwardness is joined with
sorrow at Europe's neglect of its own unique traditions defined by
the concepts of liberty, justice and the autonomous nation-state.
But instead of the 'solidarity of Europeanism' what Conrad sees is
an armed continent competing for the spoils of the earth: 'The
trouble of the civilised world is the want of a common conservative
principle abstract enough to give the impulse, practical enough to
form the rallying point of international action tending towards the
restraint of particular ambitions' (p. 111). That democracy has
'elected to pin its faith to the supremacy of material interests' (p.
107) is cited as proof of Europe's inability to benefit from the
removal of Russia's baleful influences, and since the blow against
tyranny had been struck by an eastern power, Conrad chastises
Europe's lapses by contrasting the dominant direction of its
civilisation with foreign modes in such a way that the comparison
works to the disadvantage of the contemporary West:

> The West having managed to lodge its hasty foot on the neck of
> the East is prone to forget that it is from the East that the
> wonders of patience and wisdom have come to a world of men
> who set the value of life in the power to act rather than in the
> faculty of meditation ... They [the Japanese armies] have
> created a situation in the East which they are competent to
> manage by themselves; and in doing this they have brought
> about a change in the condition of the West with which Europe
> is not well prepared to deal. The common ground of concord,
> good faith and justice is not sufficient to establish an action
> upon; since the conscience of but very few men amongst us, and
> of no single Western nation as yet, will brook the restraint of
> abstract ideas as against the fascination of a material advan-
> tage. (pp. 88, 111)

The relevance of these arguments to an analysis of *Nostromo* lies
not in Conrad's innocent reprimand of the rivalries amongst the
nations of Europe in the age of expanding capitalism nor in his
unqualified confidence in the régime of Imperial Japan, nor in the

implicit admiration of quietism, but in his lament at Europe's neglect of moral principle and relentless pursuit of economic interests. For it is an ethical faculty, and not the eastern proclivity for metaphysical speculation, that Conrad sees as the saving power the West had failed to evoke. This compound of allegiance to the traditions of a civilisation and denunciation of the opportunistic conduct degrading an inheritance enters into the novel's conception of Europeanism as both an apotheosis and a fallen state, and it is as the quintessence of high political principle that Europe confronts a foreign world devoid of ideas, standards and values.

If by representing Latin America as a casualty of foreign conquest and exploitation the fiction departs from the received version where colonisation was depicted as a blessing, then in dismissing the hybrid cultural forms of the subcontinent as the degenerate product of deleterious racial strains, *Nostromo* reproduces the conventional western view of the inborn laxity, promiscuity, immorality and incompetence afflicting whole populations. Conrad's gallery of Latin American stereotypes is set out to display an array of flaws and deficiencies in a people who are childish, cruel, irrational, sensual, pleasure-loving, ostentatious and without restraint. Whereas the sad, immobile, meek, sleepy and patient Indians, dispossessed centuries ago by the Hispanic invaders and imprisoned in their ancient mould of suffering,[7] fall outside the boundaries of the fiction's cultural conflict, the undisciplined and superstitious *mestizos*, descendants of the conquerors, the Amerindians, African slaves and white immigrants, with their instinctive love of the tawdry and their insatiable appetite for pleasure,[8] in whom European manners have been obscenely grafted on to a native base, represent violations of western norms and values. Together with their rulers, the Blanco aristocrats of pure Spanish descent cut off from their origins and frozen in an outmoded colonial style and given as are their compatriots to prevarication, oratory and emotional excess, these native Costaguaneros display the failings of the 'Southern races'. From a generalised despair at 'the levity and sufferings of that incorrigible people', the fiction focuses more closely on the tragic consequences of these vices when given rein by morally stupid, irrational, avaricious and corrupt populist politicians, motivated by impulses incomprehensible to reason, and wielding irresponsible power with singular inhumanity.

The composite picture constructed is of a continent ravished by persistent barbarism, where fatuous imbecility and blindly ferocious fanaticism characterise political life, and the succession of civil wars, conspiracies, revolutions and counter-revolutions, *pronunciamentos* and plebiscites manifest the absence of a solid foundation for stability. To lend credibility and objectivity to this narrative insistence on generic Latin American defects, the European-educated and francophile Decoud is recruited to expound a racial theory accounting for the chaos that is Latin American history:

> There is a curse of futility upon our characters: Don Quixote and Sancho Panza, chivalry and materialism, high-sounding sentiments and a supine morality, violent efforts for an idea and a sullen acquiescence in every form of corruption. We convulsed a continent for our independence only to become the passive prey of a democratic parody, the helpless victims of scoundrels and cut-throats, our institutions a mockery, our laws a farce. (p. 171)

This verdict is abundantly endorsed by the Europeans: the engineer-in-chief looks on Costaguana as a country where everything merely rational fails; Emilia Gould sees the constant changes of corrupt régimes as 'a puerile and bloodthirsty game of murder and rapine played with terrible earnestness by depraved children' (p. 49), and Charles Gould learns that 'The words one knows so well have a nightmarish meaning in this country. Liberty, democracy, patriotism, government – all of them have a flavour of folly and murder' (p. 408). Through such interpolations, a history of 'oppression and brutality' rooted in a colonial past and an imperialistic present becomes a story of racial failure and cultural deformity, and the nature of the war of the hemispheres instigated by the Hispanic conquerors and intensified by western imperialism is redefined as a contest between western standards of measure and decency and the absence of rules relating to conduct in Latin America, between the rational faculties of the Ego and the passionate energies of Id.

Because the conflict is represented as one of reason against the irrational, of law against anomie, the fiction insinuates an apologia for imperialist penetration and the ground is prepared for a blandly complimentary version of the western presence on

the subcontinent, one that foregrounds the disinterested motivation of principled Poles, Italians and Englishmen who earlier in
the century had rallied to the cause of the new and downtrodden
nations of South America fighting against the Spanish and
Portuguese Empires for the establishment of independent repub-
lics, and who had gone not as conquerors and exploiters but as
liberators, bringing with them the ideas and ideals that had
inspired the revolutions of 1848: Gould's grandfather had fought
'in the cause of independence' and Viola's formative experiences
had been with Garibaldi's army in Montevideo and on the
battle-fields of Uruguay. This account of Europe's virtuous
intervention is judiciously silent about the economic colonies
already established by the British in South America and
which, despite Gould's boast that his family's interest in America
had been motivated by 'pure love of liberty' and 'hatred of
oppression', gave the British urgent political reasons for participating in dislodging Hispanic control.[9] Indeed the fiction is at
pains to establish the idealistic dimension to the British connection with Latin America, and since the highest political principles
had been put into practice by the armies of Garibaldi who fought
against tyranny and for freedom at home and abroad, a record
which exempts them from the odium directed against the
'Southern races', the British are by legerdemain associated with
this austere republican tradition. The spiritual union between
Emilia Gould's aunt and guardian and an Italian nobleman who
had devoted his life to the independence and unity of his country
symbolises the marriage of two noble political customs, and
Viola's orotund expressions of veneration for the English single
out their sacrifice for the cause of freedom in America, dwell on his
memories of seeing 'Englishmen in the front rank of the army of
freedom' and focus on his recollection that it was an English-
woman who had given a bed to the wounded Garibaldi. But if this
selective narration of the European presence in Latin America
justifies Gould's exalted version of his family's annals and
conforms with the account preferred by historians in the West, it
is a very different incarnation of western intervention that is
animated, enunciated and denounced by the fiction, one that
aspired to conquer the earth and sought to invoke moral sanctions
for this triumphalist impulse.

The theoretical project that contrived to invest the pursuit of economic interests with spiritual attributes by decreeing worldly achievement a sacred obligation, the creation of wealth a moral duty and domination of the world the performance of God's work, is displayed in the fiction as intellectually untenable and morally reprehensible. When Conrad writes of Holroyd that he joined 'the temperament of a Puritan and an insatiable imagination of conquest' (p. 76), and disparages the 'misty idealism of the Northerners, who at the smallest encouragement dream of nothing less than the conquest of the earth' (p. 333), he illuminates in order to disavow a form of consciousness that accommodates the incommensurable and reached its full flowering in the age of imperialist expansion. With his passion for acquisition and power, Holroyd can be seen as a respectable and respected spiritual kinsman of Kurtz, like him a product of all Europe, like him a representative figure of the dominant culture in his native land. But where Kurtz ritually enacts imperialism's will to devour the cosmos, by this exceeding even the licence which colonialism had issued to itself in Africa, Holroyd's megalomania incorporates the legitimate ambitions of the most powerful of the capitalist nations and is articulated as the fulfilment of an ordained destiny:

> Time itself has got to wait on the greatest country in the whole of God's Universe. We shall be giving the word for everything: industry, trade, law, journalism, art, politics, and religion, from Cape Horn clear over to Smith's Sound, and beyond, too, if anything worth taking hold of turns up at the North Pole. And then we shall have the leisure to take in hand the outlying islands and continents of the earth. We shall run the world's business whether the world likes it or not. The world can't help it and neither can we, I guess. (p. 77)

It is well known that there are affinities between the representation of imperialism's ideology in *Nostromo* and the thesis of Conrad's contemporary Max Weber on the connection between Protestant ideas and the ethos of capitalism, which was published as essays after the writing of the novel.[10] Like Weber, Conrad distinguishes between the spirit generated in an age when technology, management and an elaborate system of moral justifications were brought to the imperialist project, and the undisguised avarice of the *conquistadores*, still a ghostly presence in Costaguana, who also sought to attach the service of God to their quest for Gold, but did not contrive to dissolve the dualism between the world of the flesh and the divine kingdom. Against the mystification of the profit motive and the idealism of economic activities – that which Decoud scorns as the faith of the market place and the stock exchange, and Emilia Gould shuns as the religion of silver and iron – the fiction's discourse mobilises a relentless attack, and the illegitimate joining of utilitarianism with idealism is condensed in the key-phrase 'material interests'.[11] Thus when the engineer-in-chief, the fiction's arch-pragmatist who himself eschews the solace of exonerating his necessary acts on ethical grounds, says about Holroyd's dream of introducing a purer form of Christianity into Latin America, 'Upon my word, doctor, things seem to be worth nothing by what they are in themselves. I begin to believe that the only solid thing about them is the spiritual value which everyone discovers in his own form of activity' (p. 318), his remarks can only be read as a sardonic commentary on the need for the self-righteous to exculpate the fault of their reprehensible deeds. The dismissive response of his companion, whose disinterested idealism allows of no concession to expediency and who insists that he puts no spiritual value in his desire, opinions or actions, confirms such an interpretation, and it is Dr Monygham's sternly-worded distinction between visible material advantage and abstract moral principle that registers the fiction's viewpoint on the flaw at the heart of the imperialist ethos.

The text's refusal to countenance the redeeming effect of idealistic intent when attached to utilitarian ends is effected in its narration of the Goulds' endeavour. Although Charles Gould, the Idealist Creator of Material Interests, invokes no religious sanction for his determination to exploit the silver mine, he, like his mentor and backer Holroyd, also nails moral purpose to the mast of economic enterprise:

> What is wanted here is law, good faith, order, security . . . I pin my faith to material interests. Only let the material interests once get a firm footing, and they are bound to impose the conditions on which alone they can continue to exist. That's how your money-making is justified here in the face of lawlessness and disorder. It is justified because the security

which it demands must be shared with an oppressed people. A
better justice will come afterwards. That's your ray of hope.
(p. 84)

This casuistic integration of piety and pragmatism, altruistic
sentiment and self-interested design, a construction which reproduces the premises of imperialist ideology, is self-exposing and is
further unmasked by Decoud's cynical estimate of Gould's
tendency to fetishise his private property and worship the result.
Yet the text itself takes a devious route in revealing Gould's moral
error by conceding his honourable commitment to an idea
detached from mercenary ambitions, while showing him to be a
man with the mind and heart of a prototypal capitalist, one whose
loyalty is not to nation, community or cause but to that which he
owns. This posture is observed by the engineer-in-chief in the
spirit of a dispassionate onlooker and not a judge, an attitude
which lends authority to his remark: 'Charles Gould . . . has said
no more about his motive than usual . . . But we all here know his
motive, and he has only one – the safety of the San Tomé mine
with the preservation of the Gould Concession in the spirit of his
compact with Holroyd' (p. 317). Despite the text's special
pleading on Gould's behalf by praising his integrity and arguing
the case for 'the conviction of practical necessity' as against
adherence to 'abstract political doctrine', what is revealed is his
readiness to stoop for his weapons as he bribes officials, backs a
régime favourable to foreign investment and, when this is
overthrown, finances the secession of Sulaco Province where his
wealth is concentrated. In the process of accounting for the
motives and actions of a man entirely devoted to his own
self-interest, the fiction's attempt to attach saving ideas to the
Goulds' financial enterprise is abandoned.

  The sacrificial victim to the delusion that purity of motive can
alter the nature of morally suspect deeds is the fiction's most
idealised protagonist, of whom it is said that her perfection of
spirit survives the sordid situations in which she is implicated.
The excess of narrative homage for Emilia Gould as compassion-
ate, fastidious, guided by an alert perception of values, wanting in
'even the most legitimate touch of materialism', inspired by
'unselfish ambitions', and 'an idealistic view of success', and able
'by the fire of her imaginative purpose' to purify the significance of
events, may appear to be a celebration of the numinous quality

which can redeem expedient acts and that can even reside in the deification of commodities:

> she had laid her unmercenary hands, with an eagerness that made them tremble, upon the first ingot turned out still warm from the mould; and by her imaginative estimate of its power she endowed the lump of metal with a justificative conception, as though it were not a mere fact, but something far-reaching and impalpable, like the true expression of an emotion or the emergence of a principle. (p. 107)

But the ultimate effect of dignifying Emilia Gould's ardent idealism is to illuminate how her nobility is perverted by complicity in reprehensible decisions and participation in idolatry, and it is the extravagance of esteem for the lady that gives edge to the many sights of her same unmercenary hands flashing with jewels which, like the silver of the San Tomé mine, had been torn manually from the earth by the labouring poor. Such images anticipate the fuller irony in Nostromo's response to her confessing hatred for the idea of the lost silver: 'Marvellous! – that one of you should hate the wealth that you know so well how to take from the hands of the poor. The world rests upon the poor, as old Giorgio says. You have always been good to the poor. But there is something accursed in wealth. Señora, shall I tell you where the treasure is? To you alone . . . Shining! Incorruptible!' (p. 560). Nostromo's speech acknowledges Mrs Gould's benign inclinations towards the dispossessed while pointing to her position as a member of that class which creates and perpetuates their condition, and by addressing her in the likeness of the silver he makes plain that just as the pure metal is tainted by its social usage, so is her virtuous personal self contaminated by her public role. The metaphor in Decoud's disclaimer, 'I am not a sentimentalist, I cannot endow my personal desire with a shining robe of silk and jewels' (p. 218), matches the repeated accounts of Mrs Gould's elegant appearance and more, it describes an imagination that transfigures base projects as noble deeds and a disposition which has need of transcribing individual gratification as disinterested concern for the commonweal; and in this light Mrs Gould's disenchantment can be seen as the outcome of her own infatuations.

To bring a political interpretation to the reading of *Nostromo* is to

confront the working out of discrepant discourses on the construction of historical meaning. The teleological view of capitalism as
the high point in human development and bourgeois democracy
as its appointed end is negated by two mutually incompatible
counter-arguments, the one belittling history as an arbitrary
series of contingent occurrences producing nothing and going
nowhere, the other reordering these same events as manifestations of processes initiated by human agency and developing
in directions determined by permutations in the strength of
competing class forces. If the chronological distortions in the first
part of the novel seem calculated, in the words of Gareth Jenkins,
to establish 'that the future does not move away from the past but
is doomed to repeat it' (op. cit., p. 149), then the encompassing
narrative arc maps the disruption of a traditional society and the
precipitate construction of a volatile and unstable new order, and
intimates the gestation of another condition beyond the historical
instance of the novel's time. It is true that in its views on history
Nostromo contradicts itself but it does so by advancing antagonistic
interpretations that are internally consistent, and whereas one
version relates the sorry tale of Costaguana's conquest, exploitation, disorder and corruption as testimony to a thesis on the
depravity of human nature and the futility of politics, the other
registers anger at the foulness of the present condition and offers a
prospect on the regenerative dimension to politics.

Since much of Costaguana's troubles and triumphs is chron-
icled by the garrulous and guileless Captain Mitchell, the text is
able openly to mock the idea of history as the linear record of
prominent persons participating in or precipitating great and
noteworthy public occurrences that coalesce to issue in the
glorious climax of progress. To this veritable Pangloss 'penetrated
by the sense of historical importance of men, events and
buildings', 'utterly in the dark, and imagining himself to be in the
thick of things', 'with a strange ignorance of the real forces at work
around him', all the signs of capitalist consolidation in Costaguana (the construction of the Railway, the reopening of the
San Tomé mine, the establishment of the Ribiera dictatorship, the
routing of the populist rebellion led by the Montero brothers, and
the foundation of the Occidental Republic to conserve the old
class system and protect imperialism's stake in the country) are
historical occasions marking an epoch, each a step in the long
struggle for Right and Justice at the Dawn of a New Era whose

coming is clearly heralded when the Treasure House of the World 'as *The Times* man calls Sulaco in his book, was saved intact for civilisation – for a great future' (p. 483). Mitchell's obtuse belief in the benign effects of imperialism and his blindness to the maturation of forces threatening its hegemony make him the obvious butt of the fiction's disdainful humour, and it is a subtler irony that is directed against the creed of the more learned but equally bemused Don José Avellanos, aristocrat and descendant of the Spanish conquerors, Blanco politician, Costaguanan patriot, diplomat, gentleman scholar and exponent of bourgeois democracy for the élite of his country: 'Don José Avellanos desired passionately for his country: peace, prosperity, and . . . "an honourable place in the comity of civilised nations". In this last phrase the Minister Plenipotentiary, cruelly humiliated by the bad faith of his Government towards the foreign bondholders, stands disclosed in the patriot' (p. 140).

The sting is in the last phrase and suggests that Avellanos's brand of patriotism is inordinately concerned with his country's good name amongst those whose interest is in exploiting its resources. When Conrad in his *Author's Note* of 1917 cites Avellanos's tome, *Fifty Years of Misrule*, as the principal authority for his own history, and in authorial intercessions refers to that work as the primary source of information about Costaguana, he is by way of a mock-earnest tone directing readers to scrutinise the writer's opinions and to recognise the gap between the principles he avers and the opportunistic means he underwrites. A scrupulous constitutionalist wedded to doctrines of political rectitude, implacably hostile to militarism, tyranny and arbitrary rule, Avellanos accepts the extraordinary powers conferred on the President-Dictator in the interests of establishing legality, good faith and order at home and redeeming 'the national credit by the satisfaction of all just claims abroad' (p. 141). The text's sceptism about Avellanos's person is civil and humane, even tempered by compassion for his illusions and the indignity of a dignified old man playing lackey to the foreign investors; but the exposure of his political ideas and policies is merciless: he dreams of modelling his country on the pattern of British democracy, but without eroding the wealth and power concentrated in the hands of the oligarchy to which he, although in straitened circumstances, belongs; his patriotism consists in appealing to the sentiment of The People while surrendering the autonomy of the country to outside interests, and when the hedonistic old soldier Barrios translates Avellanos's rhetoric into the vernacular as he assures the Europeans of the defeat of the Monterist forces, the measure of the fiction's irony towards Avellanos's innocent perfidy can be gauged:

> Señores, have no apprehension. Go on quietly making your Ferro Carril – your railways, your telegraphs. Your – There's enough wealth in Costaguana to pay for everything – or else you would not be here . . . Fear nothing, develop the country, work, work! . . . That is what Don José says we must do. Be enterprising! Work! Grow rich! To put Montero in a cage is my work; and when that insignificant piece of business is done, then, as Don José wishes, we shall grow rich, one and all, like so many Englishmen, because it is money that saves a country – (p. 164)

The fate of Avellanos's life's work, in press at the time of the civil war, is to be fired as ammunition wads which litter the plaza, float in the gutters and are trampled in the mud. With this the fiction disposes of a historical view it ideologically favours, demonstrating the casuistry of applying liberal-nationalist doctrines to a client state of imperialism dominated by a pre-industrial class hierarchy in alliance with a foreign ruling class, and where slogans of justice, patriotism and liberty and injunctions to industriousness and discipline serve the cause of the native property owners and the international investors.

Counterposed to the blandly optimistic views of those protagonists whose outlooks the fiction articulates and discredits, are the alternative and elliptical perspectives of disillusioned idealism and utopian materialism. To the first all principled political aspirations are destined to be humiliated and cruelly defeated because of the venal tendencies of the masses and the intrinsically corrupt nature of politics. The failures of the 1848 revolutions, the degeneration of the fine impulses brought to the struggles in South America and evident in Costaguana's sequence of irresponsible régimes, are cited as proof of this pessimistic perception which is endorsed by narrative interpolations on the futility of pursuing political ideals in the effort to solve political problems and the denigration of the motives to revolutions as always 'rooted in the political immaturity of the people, in the indolence of the upper classes and the mental darkness of the lower' (p. 387). Yet intersecting with this stance which recoils from the materialism of the secular world, invokes 'moral principle' and 'the idea' and rejects 'history' as the agency of regeneration, is another perspective which although unsupported by narrative sanction and obscured by a rhetoric scornful of revolutionary aims and practices, is nonetheless disseminated in the text and gathered together in a coda which cryptically acknowledges that radical politics may be the means of deliverance from an intolerable present. This viewpoint connects with the *Epigraph*, 'So foul a sky clears not without a storm', to register a prospect on the initiation of change as not only inevitable but desirable, and in this version Costaguana's history is not witnessed as an endless spiral of failure rooted in human fallibility, but as a story of successive forms of exploitation bringing into existence altered material conditions and class relationships which generate new forms of consciousness, new ambitions and new goals.

The novel begins with Sulaco, if not in a state of Edenic nature, then still in the original condition established centuries ago by the *conquistadores* and unaltered under the republic:

> In the time of Spanish rule, and for many years afterwards, the town of Sulaco — the luxuriant beauty of the orange gardens bears witness to its antiquity — had never been commercially anything more important than a coasting port with a fairly large local trade in ox-hides and indigo . . . Sulaco had found an inviolable sanctuary from the temptations of a trading world in the solemn hush of the deep Golfo Placido as if within an enormous semi-circular and unroofed temple open to the ocean, with its walls of lofty mountains hung with the mourning draperies of cloud. (p. 3)

The frontiers made by gulf and mountain define the pristine landscape on which successive cultures had acted and which it is the ambition and vocation of imperialism to destroy, and this transformation is evoked in the effacing of the primal waterfall with its symbolically primeval creatures, by the forces of progress:

> In a high ravine round the corner of the San Tomé mountain . . . the thread of a slender waterfall flashed bright and glassy through the dark green of the heavy fronds of tree-ferns. Don

Pépé, in attendance, rode up, and stretching his arm up the gorge, had declared with mock-solemnity, 'Behold the very paradise of snakes, señora.' . . . The waterfall existed no longer. The tree-ferns that had luxuriated in its spray had dried around the dried-up pool, and the high ravine was only a big trench half filled up with the refuse of excavations and tailings . . . Only the memory of the waterfall, with its amazing fernery, like a hanging garden above the rock of the gorge, was preserved in Mrs Gould's water-colour sketch. (pp. 105, 106)

But *Nostromo* is neither a lament for the passing of a primordial condition, which the fiction mistrusts for its undifferentiated substance, indifference to human desire and scorn for humanly created value, nor a eulogy to the rule of the *conquistadores* and their heirs, and the elegaic tones invoked to recall a more gracious historic past alternate with a sterner voice calling attention to the price of Sulaco's colonial elegance: 'The heavy stonework of bridges and churches left by the conquerors proclaimed the disregard of human labour, the tribute labour of vanished nations' (p. 89). For this is a story of a society built on injustice whose formal governments had changed with the establishment of a Republic and were again to alter with the coming of imperialism, but where inequality remained ingrained in the institutions. The landowners of the Campo, once warriors for the independence of Costaguana, and therefore familiar with the watchwords of Liberty and Justice, whose hospitality, dignity and breeding so impress Mrs Gould, occupy great estates with smooth-walled haciendas like fortresses, on territory expropriated centuries ago from the original inhabitants, surviving witnesses to an ancient heritage of exploitation: 'the trudging files of burdened Indians taking off their hats, would lift sad, mute eyes to the cavalcade raising the dust of the crumbling *camino real* made by the hands of their enslaved forefathers' (p. 87).

As the old relics of Spanish rule are effaced, other symbols more eloquent of the impending progress take their place, and when the equestrian statue of Charles IV is removed by the government of the Occidental Republic as an anachronism, there is talk of replacing it, in the words of Captain Mitchell, 'by a marble shaft commemorative of Separation, with angels of peace at the four corners, and bronze Justice holding an even balance, all gilt, on the top' (p. 482). By sporting with the enthusiasms of the infatuated Mitchell, the text pillories the new régime's irreverent abuse of noble ideas under whose aegis further forms of exploitation are added to the injustices of the old order. As the novel draws to a close, the narrator's reflection on the economic boom of the new Sulaco joins passing regret at a more serene past with apprehensive expectation of new possibilities, fastidious recoil from acquisitive appetites with recognition of how changes in material conditions transform the consciousness of the workers, fear of these changes and a reluctant embrace of the future this augurs:

> Sulaco outstripped Nostromo's prudence, [a reference to Nostromo's decision to grow rich slowly on the proceeds of his theft] growing rich swiftly on the hidden treasures of the earth, hovered over by the anxious spirits of good and evil, torn out by the labouring hands of the people. It was like a second youth, like a new life, full of promise, of unrest, of toil, scattering lavishly its wealth to the four corners of an excited world. Material changes swept along in the train of material interests. And other changes more subtle, outwardly unmarked, affected the minds and hearts of the workers. (p. 504)

This vision of a triumphant capitalism as the prelude to yet another social order, indeed of capitalism as breeding those who will destroy it, is fleshed out by the novel's action: the mestizos and the immigrant workers, initially willing recruits to the industrial machine and subservient to the social order underpinning it (the workers organised by Nostromo, the peasants led by a rehabilitated Hernandez and even the Indian miners from the Sierra had rallied to the defence of the Ribiera régime) now swell the ranks of the opposition Republic Party and join clandestine organisations, there is labour unrest at the mines and Dr Monygham observes that the miners would not now march on the town 'to save their Señor Administrator'. At the very moment of imperialism's victory, when the flag of Sulaco's new régime had been saluted by a United States cruiser, and the nations of progressive Europe are vying with each other to gain access to Costaguana's natural treasures, a dissident voice prophesying war against the imperialists can be heard. The speaker, Father Corbelàn, is himself the product of Costaguana's radical transformation, a witness to the alteration of the Church Militant into the Church of the Poor, for within the space of the fiction's time, the zealous proselytiser of Indians and the ardent defender of the Church's temporal powers becomes the priest who associates with secret societies and revolutionaries in the cause of reuniting Costaguana and redistributing the wealth of Sulaco concentrated in the hands of western imperialism: 'We have worked for them; we have made them, these material interests of the foreigners . . . Let them beware, then, lest the people, prevented from their aspirations, should rise and claim their share of the wealth and their share of the power' (p. 510).

The dynamics mapped by this version of history converge on the person of Nostromo and only by suppressing this dimension is it possible to read the novel as a psychological, allegorical or ethical meditation to which history is a 'context', or to interpret the eponymous protagonist as a symbolic figure tenuously connected to a social world. It is because Nostromo's transition from inchoate resentment to articulate resistance mimics a larger development in incipient class consciousness that his mythic role as slave of the treasure is an intolerable dimunition of his growing stature, and intrudes as a violation of the autonomy he had been shown to guard jealously even when objectively 'their' man. In the days of the Ribiera dictatorship he had controlled the unruly dock-workers and through the exercise of his personal authority kept labour unrest at bay; he had rallied the lightermen to the defence of the Navigation Company's property, rescued Ribiera from an outraged mob and embarked on a dangerous mission to save the silver ingots from falling into the hands of the invading Monterist forces, and even after repudiating his old function as guardian of the ruling classes, he had, this time out of deference to Viola's wishes, undertaken a dangerous journey recalling General Barrios to the defence of Sulaco and the foreign investments. Yet while still serving the property owners, Nostromo is never subservient, never abject, by his bearing and deportment appropriating an independent space within which he is his own person. Where Viola, relic of the noble nineteenth-century republican tradition, is unctuously grateful to Mrs Gould for ordinary courtesies and small favours, Nostromo maintains his distance from his masters, and when Viola thanks her for interceding with the Railway Company to guarantee his continued tenancy of the family home, Nostromo remains eloquently aloof from

the charade enacted by obsequious client and gracious bene-
factress:

> A horseman mounted on a silver-grey mare drew rein quietly in
> the shade of the house after taking off his hat to the party in the
> carriage, who returned smiles and familiar nods. Old Viola,
> evidently very pleased with the news he had just heard,
> interrupted himself for a moment to tell him rapidly that the
> house was secured, by the kindness of the English signora, for as
> long as he liked to keep it. The other listened attentively, but
> made no response.
>
> When the carriage moved on he took off his hat again, a grey
> sombrero with a silver cord and tassels . . .
>
> 'It is a great thing for me,' murmured old Giorgio, still
> thinking of the house, for now he had grown weary of change.
> 'The signora just said a word to the Englishman.'
>
> 'The old Englishman who has enough money to pay for a
> railway? . . . I've guarded his bones all the way from the
> Entrada pass down to the plain and into Sulaco, as though he
> had been my own father . . . And I have sat alone at night with
> my revolver in the Company's warehouse time and again by the
> side of that other Englishman's heap of silver, guarding it as
> though it had been my own.'
>
> Viola seemed lost in thought. 'It is a great thing for me,' he
> repeated again, as if to himself.
>
> 'It is,' agreed the magnificent Capataz de Cargadores,
> calmly. (pp. 124–5)

This scene dramatises an intersection of two political routes, with
old Viola travelling from defiance of the status quo to deference,
and Nostromo, although still sentry and strong-arm-man for the
property owners, moving in the direction that once had drawn his
mentor and surrogate-father into Garibaldi's army. Although
courteous, even courtly, in his manner towards the rich, Nostromo, in an impassivity which shows up the ignomy of the old
man's demonstrations of gratitude, announces his autonomy, just
as his replies to Viola make plain his contempt for the foreign
ruling class and his accurate estimate of the poverty of their
charity.

Here Nostromo enacts no more than a sense of moral independence but with his awakening on the mainland after the loss of the

lighter and burying the silver on the Great Isabel, a moment appropriately told as a rite of passage, his spiritual separateness from the rich is transformed into class enmity, his resentment at their 'betraying' him by burdening him with a dangerous mission which had aborted and therefore cost him his old status, offset by the knowledge that in this former existence he had betrayed his own people. But at the very moment of liberation, Nostromo is enslaved by another master, and only when the hireling who had remained a sovereign agent is overtaken by the slave of the silver does he lose his capacity for free will, submitting to the subtle seductions of the stolen ingots when he had resisted the blatant power of the oligarchs and foreigners. With this his act of defying the sacred rights of property is negated by his adopting the morality and justifications of the property owners, his righteous hatred of the emblems of exploitation vitiated by his obeisance to a symbol he despises. These confused and contradictory reactions of triumphant revenge and ignominious capitulation come together in his agonised sense of victory: 'He had defeated the spell of poverty and starvation . . . He had done it, betrayed as he was, and saving by the same stroke the San Tomé mine, which appeared to him hateful and immense, lording it by its vast wealth over the valour, over the toil, the fidelity of the poor' (pp. 502–3). The conflicting demands made by the fiction on Nostromo, who must play incompatible roles as the prototype of a growing working-class consciousness and the contemporary reincarnation of the legendary treasure-seekers, culminates when his will to social independence is overwhelmed by his mythic surrender to the silver, and even as he becomes a member of the secret societies and a fellow-traveller of the radical opposition party, so does he take spurious shelter behind the hoard of silver, 'the secret of his safety, of his influence, of his magnificence, of his power over the future, of his defiance of ill-luck, of every possible betrayal from rich and poor alike' (p. 526). Impaled by the fiction between self-determination and predestination, Nostromo desires freedom and accepts slavery, hates the rich and loves the riches, publicly castigates the ruling class and privately emulates their rituals.

All the same, in the words of the cynical Dr Monygham, he attains stature as 'the incarnation of the courage, the fidelity, the honour of "the people" ' (p. 515), and the doctor's alarm at his inexplicable influence is framed as a prophesy: 'He has genius. He is greater with the populace than ever he was before . . . that fellow has some continuity and force. Nothing will put an end to him' (pp. 511, 512). It is abundantly evident that the fiction, whose heart is with the old humanitarian revolutions of 1848, is hostile to the aspirations and practices of communism, showing the meetings of the 'good comrades' as presided over by an indignant, stickly and misshapen photographer 'with a white face and a magnanimous soul dyed crimson by a bloodthirsty hate of all capitalists, oppressors of the two hemispheres' (p. 528), and framing the critical moments in Nostromo's evolution towards radicalism against fiery and blood-stained skies. Yet cutting across these passionate disavowals, and in defiance of what is heard by Dr Monygham, who looks on what is to come with as much foreboding as he regards what is, the sound of Nostromo's name uttered by the stern and exacting Linda Viola vowing everlasting faithfulness to her faithless lover, resounds as a call to the future:

> Dr. Monygham . . . heard the name pass over his head. It was another of Nostromo's triumphs, the greatest, the most enviable, the most sinister of all. In that true cry of undying passion that seemed to ring aloud from Punta Mala to Azeuera and away to the bright line of the horizon, overhung by a big white cloud shining like a mass of solid silver, the genius of the magnificent Capataz de Cargadores dominated the dark gulf containing his conquests of treasure and love. (p. 566)

Within the rhetorical flourishes of the book's last lines, the sinister is annulled by the promise on the distant horizon, the dark offset by bright light, antinomies that are developed in the text's dual representation of The Lighthouse as the place of Nostromo's death and the emblem of social hope, and of Nostromo as both faithless lover and incorruptible figurehead, thief tied to a horde of silver and radical contemptuous of this symbol of property. In the end Nostromo survives his abject capitulation to live on in the minds and hearts of Costaguana's poor as exemplar of their aspirations. With this the formal design of a novel informed by a viewpoint fearful of historical change is altered by the text's irresolute embrace of excluded tendencies as the bleak pessimism of the fiction's discourse and conscious outlook is irradiated by intimations of a transfigured future.

Conclusion

The profound hypocrisy and inherent barbarism of bourgeois civilisation lies unveiled before our eyes, turning from its home, where it assumes respectable forms, to the colonies, where it goes naked.
Karl Marx: 'Future Results of British Rule in India', 1853

. . . we in Europe too are being decolonised . . . Let us look at ourselves, if we can bear to, and see what is becoming of us. First, we must face that unexpected revelation, the strip-tease of our humanism. There you can see it, quite naked, and it's not a pretty sight. It was nothing but an ideology of lies, a perfect justification for pillage; its honeyed words, its affectation of sensibility were only alibis for our aggressions.
Jean-Paul Sartre: *Preface* to Frantz Fanon, *The Wretched of the Earth*, 1961

British fiction at the turn of the century had been inundated on its periphery with a large output of best-selling colonial romances vaunting the prodigious qualities and achievements of an imperial nation. More centrally, it had been penetrated by Kipling's ambivalent celebrations of empire where fascination with the exercise of domination over nature and people was in conflict with mixed perceptions of colonialism's historical meanings. In a situation where imperialism had been naturalised by fiction, Conrad's writings, which refused legitimacy to the imperialist vocation, entered literature as a protest against the canonical account of its intent and destination. Because he lived on the borderlines of various traditions, Conrad occupied a vantage point beyond the outlook of disaffected political writers who like him reviled the materialism of their society, deplored the motives of a ruthless colonialism and were alarmed at the flagrant chauvinism this had excited, but believed imperialism to be a malaise within capitalism – J. A. Hobson's study of imperialism was subtitled 'A Study of Social Pathology'[1] – and retained faith in liberal democracy to regain the ground lost to the new ethos. Marxist theoreticians were subsequently to demonstrate that far from being a passing morbid condition, imperialism was an intrinsic extension of capitalism and a revelation of its depravity. But at the time that Conrad was writing, when moderate British socialists had aligned themselves with the protagonists of empire in formulating a Fabian imperialism and only lone voices spoke out against capitalist-national imperialism as a threat to international Social-Democracy,[2] the debate in Britain about imperialism was dominated by the liberal radicals. Always scrupulous in acknowledging the virtues of a beneficent or genuine imperialism, which they justified in terms of a moral responsibility owing to low-type and unprogressive races and the necessity of utilising the earth's resources in the interests of international efficiency, these enemies of empire directed their critique at the disagreeable features of a mischievous and exploitative colonialism. For them the reigning imperialist temperament which suspended considerations of morality when ratifying territorial expansion and condoned the ill-treatment of 'backward populations', had the effect of stimulating national conceit and fostering militarism, thereby poisoning the mind and character of the British people and posing a danger to democracy in the modern nation state.[3] They argued that the current phase of imperialism had been instigated by sectarian and self-seeking interests like those of financiers, stock-jobbers and war contractors who, deprived of investment possibilities at home, sought outlets for the export of surplus capital, and claimed that the solution lay in the redistribution of income in the metropolitan country, that is in the reform of the existing economic and social structure.

Thus while liberal critics of empire defended the principles of bourgeois humanism against the aggressive tendencies of a rabid colonialism, Conrad's fictions, which represent the victory of the new values as a sign of a bankrupt social order, reveal imperialist theology as a facet of capitalism's ideology. Having independently detected the triumphalist direction of western civilisation to which Spengler ascribed its transformation and impending decline, Conrad brought to this recognition an apprehension of imperialism as the last and most degraded stage in the history of a social system, and in the fiction the foremost imperial city, the centre of colonial trade and the junction to the traffic of international finance capital, *is* a heart of darkness:

> The air was dark above Gravesend, and farther back still seemed condensed into a mournful gloom, brooding motionless over the biggest, and the greatest, town on earth . . . The offing was barred by a black bank of clouds, and the tranquil waterway leading to the uttermost ends of the earth flowed sombre under an overcast sky – seemed to lead into the heart of an immense darkness. (*Heart of Darkness*, pp. 45, 162)

In writings that are addressed as admonition and entreaty to the peoples of the imperialist nations, atonement for the despondency of this vision is made by projecting images of the future, and negative representations of those fixed standards, immutable precepts and scriptural legends underpinning the established order are juxtaposed to intimations of a prospective time still to be occupied by other forms of human society devoted to the attainment of alternative ends. If this vatic impulse to Conrad's writings is acknowledged, then the interpretations of critics attempting to establish his credentials as a reluctant disciple of the official ethos would seem to be suspect and insupportable. The most assertive of such arguments claims that it was Conrad's intention to direct his readers firmly back to 'duty and sacrifice and a familiar morality of action . . . All that Conrad could offer . . . was fidelity to simple ideas and a highly pragmatic idealism' (Alan Sandison, op. cit., pp. 130, 138). Any analysis of Conrad's fictions that finds in them a regretful advocacy of surrender to the God of Things as They Are, derives from a resolutely literal reading of texts which is blind to the dialectic of discourses where conservative principles are enunciated only to be negated, insensible to irony and deaf to the many voices defying the authority of the status quo. This present study has been concerned with discussing Conrad's works as ideologically constituted perceptions of history that interrogate the premises of the authorised version. But since rejection of imperialism's orthodox values generates a search for its unrealised ideals and, when this is abandoned, for an emergent and wholly dissimilar condition, the method of interpretation had necessarily to accommodate the texts' production of meanings beyond ideology.

Even where the past is recreated as a golden age of sublime

ambitions and herculean feats and colonial myth appears to be endorsed, what is honoured is the human capacity to transcend a prospect restricted by existing conditions and to initiate history. It is this faculty that Marlow acknowledges when he applauds the 'bizarre obstinacy of that desire' which had induced the traders of old to defy danger and death not simply to acquire riches, but 'in obedience to an inward voice, to an impulse beating in the blood, to a dream of the future' (*Lord Jim*, p. 227). So too the discovery of saving ideas and great illusions which transfigure the practice of those who participate in morally indefensible projects is a tribute to the pursuit of exalted objectives in the real world and not a confirmation that these can be consummated within existing conditions. The status of the redeeming idea as a positive force in transforming dubious situations is never more than uncertain in the fictions, and with *Lord Jim* the exercise of the visionary imagination in prefiguring forms and values that have not yet come into being is celebrated as an indispensable human attribute. Here the dream [" 'That was the way. To follow the dream and again to follow the dream' " (pp. 214–15)] is conceived as the inspiration to the ultimate realisation of social goals. There is evidence in Conrad's essays and letters that he mistrusted misty idealism and feared the consequences of trafficking with utopian images, and in such contexts they stand uncontradicted as articles of faith. But when repeated in the fictions, the denigrations engender their own opposites, and even as millenarianism is censured, so is the chiliastic urge affirmed as an intrinsic and significant category of human feeling. Where given conditions limit the fulfilment of the wish, visionary desire is a protest agianst this curtailment and a zone of freedom won back from the tyranny of circumstances; the striving after 'horizons as boundless as hope, the quest for the Ever-undiscovered country' (*Lord Jim*, p. 338) is not an escape from history but a route towards its making.

The representation of human renewal through rebellion against the insufficiencies and constraints of the existing world culminates in *Nostromo*. Here the importuning of a lost Edenic state meets with no validation in history, and since the critique of a social order founded on the sanctity of property precludes the project of attaching ethical purpose to pragmatic ends, the past cannot be recovered as an exemplary moral order, nor the present redeemed by the discovery of its concealed idealistic character. The repudiation of a civilisation which lays claim to be the pinnacle and appointed end of human history makes space for the invocation of an eschatology inimical to the imperialist world-view, one that foresees not finalities but endless tomorrows on the far horizons. As the search for redemptive features within a world made by imperialism is displaced by hope deferred to the future, the pessimistic perspective of fictions which represent late bourgeois civilisation as a fallen state is illuminated by the optimism of the will to anticipate what is still missing in human conditions.

Notes

1. See *Conrad: The Critical Heritage*, edited Norman Sherry (London: Routledge and Kegan Paul, 1973).
2. See *Joseph Conrad's Letters to R. B. Cunninghame Graham*, edited C. T. Watts (Cambridge: Cambridge University Press, 1969). On 8 February 1899 Conrad wrote to Cunninghame Graham about the latter's enthusiastic response to the first instalments of *Heart of Darkness*: 'I am simply in seventh heaven to find you like the 'Heart of Darkness' so far. You bless me indeed. Mind you don't curse me by and bye for the very same thing. There are two more instalments in which the idea is so wrapped up in secondary notions that you – even you! – may miss it' (p. 116).
3. Edward Said in *Orientalism* (London: Routledge and Kegan Paul, 1978) categorises Orientalism as a western style for dominating, restructuring and having authority over the Orient and sets out to show 'how European culture gained in strength and identity by setting itself off against the Orient as a sort of surrogate and even underground self' (p. 3).
4. S. S. Prawer in *Karl Marx and World Literature* (Oxford: Oxford University Press, 1976), rescues Marx's conception of literature as 'a token of the human capacity for free creation' from the obloquy of determinism attributed to it by hostile critics, showing how Marx distinguished between class ideology and the free intellectual or spiritual production of writers and thinkers who place themselves in opposition to the dominant modes of thought (pp. 313–14).
5. 'Henry James: An Appreciation' (1905) in *Notes on Life and Letters* (1921), p. 15.
6. Letter to *New York Times*, dated 29 August 1901, quoted in Lawrence Graver, *Conrad's Shorter Fictions* (California: University of California Press, 1969), pp. 43–4.
7. For discussion of the relations between English and foreign experience in Conrad's writings, see Terry Eagleton, *Exiles and Emigrés* (London: Chatto and Windus, 1970).
8. 'Autocracy and War' (1905) in *Notes on Life and Letters*, pp. 88, 111.
9. See, for example, Christine Bolt, *Victorian Attitudes to Race* (London: Routledge and Kegan Paul, 1971); Brian V. Street, *The Savage in Literature: Representations of 'primitive' society in English Fiction 1858–1920* (London: Routledge and Kegan Paul, 1975); and Marion Berghahn, *Images of Africa in Black American Literature* (London: Macmillan, 1977).
10. The polarities in interpretations of black/dark in Conrad's fiction are

instructive: Royal Roussel in *The Metaphysics of Darkness* (Baltimore: Johns Hopkins, 1971), reads the dark wholly as a metaphor for the primal ground of existence and ultimate reality; in contrast J. C. Echeruo argues that Conrad's use of blackness is culturally conditioned and meets audience expectations, see *The Conditioned Imagination From Shakespeare to Conrad: Studies in the Exo-cultural Stereotype* (London: Macmillan, 1978).

11. See Eloise Knapp Hay, *The Political Novels of Joseph Conrad: A Critical Study* (Chicago: The University of Chicago Press, 1963); Avrom Fleishman, *Conrad's Politics: Community and Anarchy in the Fiction of Joseph Conrad* (Baltimore: Johns Hopkins, 1967); Terry Eagleton, *Exiles and Emigrés* (London: Chatto and Windus, 1970) and *Criticism and Ideology: A Study in Marxist Literary Theory* (London: New Left Books, 1976); Jeremy Hawthorn, *Joseph Conrad: Language and Fictional Self-consciousness* (London: Edward Arnold, 1979); Ian Watt, *Conrad in the Nineteenth Century* (London: Chatto and Windus, 1980); and Fredric Jameson, *The Political Unconscious: Narrative as a Socially Symbolic Act* (London: Methuen, 1981).

12. This tendency, observable since Conrad's centenary in the mid-1950s, elicited a protest from Douglas Hewitt in the 1968 edition of an earlier study, where he reiterated his belief that the metaphoric effects of Conrad's work are rooted in the literal world. It also prompted Raymond Williams, in an argument that makes the distinction between discovering a general truth in a particular situation, and making an abstract truth out of a contingent one, to dispute that critical tradition which reduces deliberately created realities to analogies, symbolic circumstances and abstract situations. See Douglas Hewitt, *Conrad: A Reassessment* (London: Bowes and Bowes, 1968, first published 1952) and Raymond Williams 'Conrad' in *The English Novel From Dickens to Lawrence* (London: Chatto and Windus, 1971).

13. This discussion subsumes a variety of methodological approaches: in *The Wheel of Empire: A Study of the Imperial Idea in Some Late Nineteenth and Early Twentieth Century Fiction* (London: Macmillan, 1967), Alan Sandison argues that in fictions which were morally but not ideologically connected to imperialism, the imperial idea offered 'in its innate tensions, a moral correlative for the exploration of the antithesis between consciousness and the hostile principle by which it is menaced' (pp. 120–1). Sandison's insistence that ideology played no part in the politics of imperialism, and his preoccupation with demonstrating the writers' commitment to action and self-consciousness as the means to securing identity and integrity, leads him to overlook Conrad's ambivalent relationship to the imperial idea, reading his doubts as affirmations and his ironies as ethical prescriptions. Jeffrey Meyers in *Fiction and the Colonial Experience* (Ipswich: The Boydell Press, 1973), interprets the fictions as explorations of the cultural conflict inherent in the colonial situation, commending the 'valuable humanistic approach to the problems of colonialism' evinced by the authors. For him Conrad's writings express a consistent viewpoint on colonialism and unproblematically demonstrate that civilised values and moral principle are incompatible with material interests. D. C. R. A. Goonetilleke, *Developing Countries in British Fiction* (London: Macmillan, 1977) deals with the fictions as representations of historical circumstances and reflections of prevalent racial attitudes. In *The Colonial Encounter: a reading of six novels* (London: Rex

Collings, 1977) M. M. Mahood is concerned to connect historical thinking on imperialism and the end of empire with selected works of fiction as creations of a particular historical imagination. Her interpretation of *Heart of Darkness* as a mesh of intellectual attitudes and responses to the colonial experience locates two narrative viewpoints, the one exposing colonial exploitation, the other affirming belief in the beneficence of English imperialism and the notion of trusteeship. Because Jonah Raskin's *The Mythology of Imperialism* (New York: Random House, 1971) was written in the transient style of the hippy counter-culture, it did not receive the serious attention it deserves, for despite its wayward delivery and occasional salutes to irrationalism, it does dramatically demonstrate how the fictions produce contradictory ideological positions. His discussion of Conrad centres on the writer's apprehensions of imperialism as a state of crisis and conflict, but because he does not look at the origins and designs of Conrad's inconsistent perspectives, he celebrates rather than analyses the fictions' contradictions. In *Dreams of Adventure, Deeds of Empire* (London: Routledge and Kegan Paul, 1980), Martin Green maps a literary tradition remote from high culture, locating in adventure tales the energising myths of English imperialism. He tends to reduce Conrad's noted ambivalence to the joining of a sceptical, ironic view of adventure with an endorsement of its values, which he faults as being effected through the lavish and clumsy use of its characteristic motifs. John A. McClure in *Kipling and Conrad: The Colonial Fiction* (Cambridge, Mass. and London: Harvard University Press, 1981) approaches the colonial fictions of the two authors as chronicles of the extinct world of the colonialist which undercuts the romantic image of the life and reveals the contradictions in the colonial situation. He argues that whereas Kipling endorses his dramatisations of the authoritarian disposition developed in imperialism's servants, Conrad maintains a critical stance towards the imperialist ambition. The existence of a truly meretricious book in this subgenre must be mentioned: Robert F. Lee in *Conrad's Colonialism* (The Hague and Paris: Mouton, 1969), recruits Conrad as an ally in his own contempt for the non-European world by asserting that the direction of Conrad's fiction is to question the colonial peoples' fitness for independence.

14. *Studies in the Theory of Imperialism* (Proceedings of a Seminar held at Oxford 1969/70), edited Roger Owen and Bob Sutcliffe (London: Longman, 1972). See also V. G. Kiernan, *Marxism amd Imperialism* (London: Edward Arnold, 1974). For a summary of the variations in usage, see Raymond Williams, *Keywords* (London: Fontana, 1976), pp. 131–2.

15. Thomas Hodgkin, 'Some African and Third World Theories of Imperialism', in *Studies in the Theory of Imperialism*, op. cit. In this connection, the writings of Frantz Fanon are of central importance.

16. Gareth Jenkins, 'Conrad's *Nostromo* and History', *Literature and History*, No. 6 (Autumn 1977). See also Stephen Zelnick, 'Conrad's *Lord Jim*: Meditations on the Other Hemisphere', *The Minnesota Review*, No. 11 (Fall 1978) who seeks to correct the location of the issues of imperialism 'out there' or in special moments of conflict:

'Far less attention is paid to the origin of modern imperialism and the structural distortions of the metropolitan community: the dislocation of community traditions and identity; the mystified presentation of social power as administrative routine; the reduction of work to abstract function within a leviathanic order not easily comprehended and systematically disguised; and, the projection of delusive ideologies that produce confusion in those who try to live by them' (p. 77).

17. For a succinct discussion of how ideology has been conceived within the Marxist tradition, see Tony Bennett, *Formalism and Marxism* (London: Methuen, 1979).

18. See Hugh Cunningham, 'The Language of Patriotism, 1790–1914', *History Workshop*, Issue 12 (Autumn 1981), p. 24.

19. Raymond Williams, 'Problems of Materialism', in *Problems in Materialism and Culture* (London: Verso Editions and New Left Books, 1980), p. 110.

20. Even in a journal traditionally critical of colonialism, a reviewer has within the past decade written: 'In simple terms . . . Empire tried to do good and to keep the peace for a hundred years. Whether the world is a better place for its passing is a matter of opinion; only a bigot could deny that the world was a better place for its existence. 'Keeping the Map Pink', review of James Morris, *Farewell the Trumpets: An Imperial Retreat*, by George MacDonald Fraser, *New Statesman*, 29 September 1978, p. 412. The assumptions behind this statement have affinities with those informing the discussion on the 'balance-sheet of imperialism' as conducted by western academics and in which the benefits of modernisation and efficiency outweigh the negative experiences of colonialism known by the colonised. See for example D. W. Brogan, 'Re-thinking Imperialism', *Encounter*, May 1960, and Rupert Emerson, 'Colonialism' in *The Journal of Contemporary History*, 4, No 1 (1969), an issue devoted to *Colonialism and Decolonisation*.

21. Letter to Aniela Zagorska, dated 25 December 1899, quoted by Zdzislaw Najder, *Conrad's Polish Background* (London: Oxford University Press, 1964) p. 232.

22. Letter to William Blackwood dated 31 December 1898 in *Joseph Conrad: Letters to William Blackwood and David S. Meldrum*, edited William Blackburn (North Carolina: Duke University Press, 1958), pp. 36–7.

23. Cedric Watts and Laurence Davies, *Cunninghame Graham: A Critical Biography* (Cambridge: Cambridge University Press, 1979).

24. While criticising Cunninghame Graham's lack of control in 'Bloody Niggers', published in *Social Democrat*, April 1897, Conrad was in sympathy with the savage attack it launched on the pretensions of British imperialism. See *Letters to R. B. Cunninghame Graham* (op. cit.).

25. See Terry Eagleton, *Criticism and Ideology* (op. cit.):

English society itself offered Conrad an ideal resolution of the conflicting ideological imperatives he inherited from his Polish context; it became a welcome enclave for the conservative *émigré* in flight from European political turbulence. Its tolerant, pragmatic individualism united with the organic, Romantic nationalist heritage of the merchant service to provide Conrad with precisely the ideological conjuncture he sought. (p. 133)

26. See 'Autocracy and War' (1905) and 'The Crime of Partition' (1919) in *Notes on Life and Letters*.

27. 'As to the peace meeting. If you want me to come I want still more to hear

you. But – I am not a peace man, not a democrat (I don't know what the word means really) . . . I cannot admit the idea of fraternity not so much because I believe it impracticable, but because its propaganda (the only thing really tangible about it) tends to weaken the national sentiment the preservation of which is my concern . . . International fraternity may be an object to strive for . . . but that illusion imposes by its size alone.' Letter dated 8 February 1899 in *Letters to R. B. Cunninghame Graham*, pp. 116–17. In the essay 'The Heroic Age', *The Mirror of the Sea* (1906), Conrad reiterates his sentiments on the national spirit in phrases more sonorous and sententious than those used in the letter:

> In the ceaseless rush of shadows and shades, that, like the fantastic forms of clouds cast darkly upon the waters on a windy day, fly past us to fall headlong below the hard edge of an implacable horizon, we must turn to the national spirit, which, superior in its force and continuity to good and evil fortune, can alone give us the feeling of an enduring existence, and of an invincible power against the fates. Like a subtle and mysterious elixir poured into the perishable clay of successive generations, it grows in truth, splendour and potency with the march of ages. In its incorruptible flow round the globe of the earth it preserves from decay and forgetfulness of death the greatness of our great men, and amongst them the passionate and gentle greatness of Nelson, the nature of whose genius was, on the faith of a brave seaman and distinguished Admiral, such as to 'Exalt the glory of our nation.' (p. 194)

28. Author's Note to *A Personal Record* (1912) where Conrad distinguishes between revolts against foreign domination and subversion of existing political systems (pp. ix–x).
29. Conrad's reiterations of the racist non-science prevalent at the turn of the century which equated a primitive technology with irrational thinking, and his spontaneous embrace of the anti-semitism inherited from his ancestral environment, should have assisted him in feeling at home amongst his social peers in his adopted country, just as his excursions in the writing of patriotic encomiums must have endeared him to his hosts. Those scholars who consider it churlish, priggish and anachronistic to acknowledge that famous writers held opinions that are now considered to be ill-founded, offensive and socially dangerous, avoid looking at the ways in which such views are part of an ideological formation and enter as thesis or antithesis in the working out of the fictions' dialectic.
30. Najder, op. cit., p. 31.
31. See as examples 'Tradition' (1918) in *Notes on Life and Letters*.
32. See 'Well Done' (1918), ibid.
33. 'Books' (1905), ibid.
34. The most comprehensive listing of the extensive literature on Conrad up to 1971 is Bruce E. Teets and Helmut E. Gerber, *Joseph Conrad: An Annotated Bibliography of Writings About Him* (De Kalb: North Illinois University Press, 1971). *Conradiana* carries regular listings of new work on Conrad.
35. Jacques Berthoud, *Joseph Conrad: The Major Phase* (Cambridge: Cambridge University Press, 1978), p. 4.
36. Frederick Karl, *Joseph Conrad: The Three Lives* (London: Faber, 1979).

37. Ian Watt, *Conrad in the Nineteenth Century* (London: Chatto and Windus, 1980).

38. Frederick Karl, 'Conrad Studies', review essay in *Studies in the Novel*, 9, No 3 (Fall 1977), pp. 326–7.

39. V. S. Naipaul, 'Conrad's Darkness' in *The Return of Eva Peron* (London: Deutsch, 1980).

40. If Chinua Achebe's blunt attack on *Heart of Darkness* dispenses with the recognised language of critical discourse, his protest at Conrad's insulting representations of Africa should be listened to by critics for the 'truth' this registers:

> I have no doubt that the reason for the high rating of this novel in Europe and America is simply that there it fortifies fears and prejudices and is clever enough to protect itself, should the need arise, with the excuse that it is not really about Africa at all. And yet it is set in Africa and teems with Africans whose humanity is admitted in theory but totally undermined by the mindlessness of its context and the pretty explicit animal imagery surrounding it. ('Viewpoint', *Times Literary Supplement*, No 4010, 1 February 1980, p. 113)

Against this expression of outrage, the plea that it would be insensitive to let the 'rather smug cultural relativism of our own age' distort our reading of *Heart of Darkness*, see M. M. Mahood, op. cit., p. 27, itself appears rather insensitive and smug.

41. 'Books', op. cit., pp. 5–6.

CHAPTER 2: *Heart of Darkness*

1. Written for and serialised in the pro-imperialist *Blackwood's Magazine* in 1899, the novella was enthusiastically received both by advocates and by opponents of empire and colonial expansion; see *Joseph Conrad: Letters to William Blackwood and David S. Meldrum*, edited W. Blackburn (North Carolina: Duke University Press, 1958) and *Joseph Conrad's Letters to R. B. Cunninghame Graham*, edited C. T. Watts (Cambridge University Press, 1969).

2. See *Joseph Conrad: An Annotated Bibliography of Writings About Him*, compiled by Bruce Teets and Helmut Gerber (De Kalb: North Illinois University Press, 1971). Although the mainstream of current critical discussion is not concerned with the work's ideological representations, the consensus is that it contains a 'public dimension' and that this is directed at exposing a particular phase and form of imperialism. For samples of the discourse, see *Joseph Conrad's 'Heart of Darkness' Backgrounds and Criticism*, edited Leonard F. Dean (New Jersey: Prentice Hall, 1960); *The Art of Joseph Conrad: A Critical Symposium*, edited R. W. Stallman (East Lansing: Michigan State University Press, 1960); *'Heart of Darkness': An Authoritative Text, Backgrounds and Sources: Essays in Criticism*, edited Robert Kimbrough (New York: Norton, 1963); C. T. Watts, *Conrad's 'Heart of Darkness': A Critical and Contextual Discussion* (Milan: Mursia International, 1977). In 'Conrad's Critique of Imperialism

in *Heart of Darkness'*, *PMLA* 94, No. 2 (1979), Hunt Hawkins impressively musters the historical context to the fiction, which he considers to be a condemnation of imperialism; his interpretative commentary, however, suffers from a tendency to a reductive approach. In 'Imperialism: Conrad's *Heart of Darkness'*, *Journal of Contemporary History*, 2, No. 2 (1967), issue entitled *Literature and Society*, Jonah Raskin discusses the novella as a myth about imperialist decadence, and John McClure, 'The Rhetoric of Restraint: *Heart of Darkness'*, *Nineteenth Century Fiction*, 32, No. 3 (1977), argues that the work explores the rhetoric of the passion for domination inherent in late nineteenth-century imperialism and juxtaposes this to the ethic of self-restraint.

3. *Letters to Blackwood and Meldrum*, pp. 36–7. For information on Conrad's Congo experiences, see 'The Congo Diary' (1925) and 'Geography and Some Explorers' (1924) in *Last Essays* (1926), and Gérard Jean-Aubry, *Joseph Conrad in the Congo* (New York: Haskell House, 1973, first published 1926). It was in 'Geography and Some Explorers' that Conrad referred to colonial ventures in the Congo as 'the vilest scramble for loot that ever disfigured the history of human conscience and geographical exploration' (p. 25).

4. These dualistic configurations all but obscure a parallel pattern alluding to the connections between the two hemispheres: grass growing over bones in Africa, grass growing through stones in Brussels, or the identical gestures of Kurtz's barbarous black woman and his ethereal and fair Intended. It is, however, difference rather than affinity that the fiction explores.

5. The most obvious and best-known example of black and white locked into their imperialist meanings is *The White Man's Burden*:

> Take up the White Man's burden –
> And reap his old reward:
> The blame of those ye better,
> The hate of those ye guard –
> The cry of hosts ye humour
> (Ah, slowly!) toward the light: –
> 'Why brought ye us from bondage,
> 'Our loved Egyptian night?' (Kipling, 1899)

6. Cf. Conrad's remark regarding *Heart of Darkness* in the Author's Note to *'Youth': A Narrative and Two Other Stories* appended in 1917, where he compares its mode of writing to that of *Youth*: 'it is experience pushed a little (and only a very little) beyond the actual facts of the case for the perfectly legitimate, I believe, purpose of bringing it home to the minds and bosoms of the readers. There it was no longer a matter of sincere colouring. It was like another art altogether. That sombre theme had to be given a sinister resonance, a tonality of its own, a continued vibration that, I hoped, would hang in the air and dwell on the ear after the last note had been struck' (p. xi).

7. The 'realistic' descriptions in the manuscript version of decomposing colonialist pretensions in the shape of demoralised white men in seedy once-grand hotels are absent from the published form where it is the fantastic quality of European's invasion and punishment that predominates. See Kimbrough, op. cit.

8. Marlow's narration draws attention to the helmsman, the harlequin, Kurtz's adorers, his woman and his Intended expressing themselves precisely and eloquently through looks, gestures and sounds, an emphasis which denigrates the spoken word. All the same he hears African speech as not human, assumes the notes made by the Russian sailor in the manual on seamanship to be written in cipher, and craves conversation with Kurtz because he speaks English, thus demonstrating his dependence on a known language.

9. For a discussion on the idea of the supreme value of work, see Ian Watt, '*Heart of Darkness* and Nineteenth-Century Thought', *Partisan Review*, XLV (1978).

10. There are other instances of Marlow's failure to register the ironies implicit in what he says: having made plain that rapacious colonialism is a continental venture in which Britain is a senior partner, he expresses himself gratified at seeing a vast amount of red on the map 'because one knows that some real work is being done in there' (p. 55). Nor does he disclose the further implications to his sardonic account of Kurtz's ancestry and upbringing: 'The original Kurtz had been educated partly in England, and – as he was good enough to say himself – his sympathies were in the right place' (p. 117).

11. In ' "Gnawed Bones" and "Artless Tales": Eating and Narrative in Conrad', Tony Tanner writes of *Heart of Darkness*: 'This is a study of a certain kind of white imperial consciousness which, as it were, wants to engorge the world and transform it into self'. See *Joseph Conrad: A Commemoration: Papers for the 1974 International Conference on Conrad*, edited Norman Sherry (London: Macmillan, 1976), p. 32.

12. In *The Savage in Literature: Representations of 'primitive' society in English Fiction 1858–1920* (London: Routledge and Kegan Paul, 1975), Brian V. Street shows that many of the stereotypes about 'primitive' life had hardened even before the scramble for Africa and that 'imperialists tended to use theories already worked out by scientists and which lent themselves to political manipulation'. Street gives a telling summary of the image devised in anthropological studies: 'Primitive peoples are considered to be slaves of custom and thus unable to break the despotism of their own "collective consciousness". Any custom "discovered" among a "primitive" people is assumed to dominate their whole lives; they are unconscious of it and will never change it themselves. This provides the basis for the analysis of many customs being reported back to nineteenth-century England by the growing number of travellers' (pp. 5, 6).

13. Cf. K. K. Ruthven, 'The Savage God: Conrad and Lawrence', *Critical Quarterly*, X, Nos. 1 and 2 (1968), who appears to concur with the construction devised by the 'fin de siècle Decadent Movement' about savage primitivism possessing a 'pre-logical consciousness' and fostering the 'whole man' repressed and dismembered by civilisation.

14. It is Ruthven's argument, ibid., that concealed behind Marlow's overt disapproval is a cautious and evasive case for Kurtz, a strategic celebration of his achievement in transcending civilisation's restraints and repressions.

15. In Marlow's perceptions of Africa, the 'primitive' is associated with some postulated 'pre-human' condition that is lawless and irrational. Although there is evidence that Conrad shared this view, the fiction opens up such

assumptions to question, and present-day critics who continue to ascribe the dislocation of white protagonists to the unconscious, mindless and uncaring immensity of the Non-European cosmos, are uncritically perpetuating that ethnic solipsism which Conrad's fictions register but interrogate.

16. Cf. John A. McClure, 'The Rhetoric of Restraint in *Heart of Darkness*', op. cit., who contrasts the passion for domination reflected in Kurtz's speech with Marlow's restrained and probing manner of address, which he sees as 'a symbolic manifestation of his ethos of self-restraint' (p. 312). The argument in the present discussion is that Marlow and Kurtz represent variations within one consciousness, against which is posed the consciousness of the other hemisphere.

17. In the manuscript version, the sentence 'It could only be obtained by conquest – or surrender', follows 'We were cut off from comprehension of our surroundings'. See Kimbrough, op. cit., p. 36.

18. The converging crowds carrying spears, bows and shields, casting wild glances, making savage movements and uttering weird cries, the dark shapes in fantastic headdresses and spotted skins, standing warlike and still in statuesque repose, are amongst the many clichés used by Conrad and later adopted by popular 'epic' films set in Africa.

19. In his reading of the fiction, Jeremy Hawthorn, op. cit., contrasts Conrad's suspicion of eloquence with his trust in technical language as a register of truth and reality.

CHAPTER 3: *The Rescue: A Romance of the Shallows*

1. Vernon Young, 'Lingard's Folly: The Lost Subject', *Kenyon Review*, 15 (1953), dismisses the novel as the most egregrious of Conrad's failures; Thomas Moser, ' "The Rescuer" Manuscript: A Key to Conrad's Development – and Decline', *Harvard Library Bulletin* (Autumn 1956), argues that the finished work demonstrates an atrophy of Conrad's symbolic imagination; and Frederick Karl, *Joseph Conrad: The Three Lives* (London: Faber, 1979), considers it suffers from a 'potpourri of mannerisms' and that in terms of his career Conrad would have done better to let it lie dormant. Eloise Knapp Hay, *The Political Novels of Joseph Conrad* (Chicago: University of Chicago Press, 1963), does pay the novel serious attention in discussing it as a political fable about relations between East and West, and Avrom Fleishman, *Conrad's Politics: Community and Anarchy in the Fiction of Joseph Conrad* (Baltimore: Johns Hopkins, 1967), approaches it as a tragic interpretation of the Rajah Brooke myth, but does not deal with the literary realisation of this theme. Gareth Jenkins, 'Conrad's *Nostromo* and History' in *Literature and History*, No. 6 (Autumn 1977), maintains that Conrad sidestepped the question of imperialism in the novel and attributes Conrad's writing difficulties to an inability to deal with the ideological problem: 'just how was he to understand and depict metropolitan society, the nature of its interrelationships, the nature of its relationship to other societies – in short, its complex imperialist structure?' (p. 139).

2. Cf. the cruder approach to the antagonisms as between two degraded

worlds, the degenerate European and the barbaric native, in *Almayer's Folly* and *An Outcast of the Islands.*

3. Ashley Library 4787, British Museum.

4. Conrad's letters make repeated reference to the difficulties he was experiencing with the novel. Little of the alternately inert and overheated material written in 1916 found its way into the completed work; this covers the time when Edith Travers and Lingard make their way during a storm from the shoals to the Shore of Refuge and charts the growth of their intimacy.

5. The shifts in the conception of Lingard leave the basic contours of the characterisation intact, whereas the incompletely effected alterations in the portrayal of Mrs Travers result in capricious inconsistencies. In 'The Rescuer', where she is referred to as Edith Travers, sympathy for her person and plight as an idealist cheated of a cause is repeatedly invited; in *The Rescue* she has become Mrs Travers, an appellation imposing a distance which is further established by allusions to her brittle and disingenuous nature, although admiration for her charm, intelligence and honesty continues to be solicited. Conrad's own enchantment with this figure of his imagination is apparent from his remark to Edward Garnett in a letter written on 11 July 1920, commenting on a criticism which had been made of her conceptualisation in a review: 'I cared too much for Mrs Travers to play pranks with her on the lines of heroics or tenderness; and being afraid of striking a false note I failed to do her justice – not so much in action, I think, as in expression'. (Gérard Jean-Aubry, *Joseph Conrad: Life and Letters* (London: Heinemann, 1927) II, pp. 243–4.)

6. 'The worst is that while I am thus powerless to produce, my imagination is extremely active: whole paragraphs, whole pages, whole chapters pass through my mind. Everything is there: descriptions, dialogue . . . reflexion – everything – everything but the belief, the conviction, the only thing needed to make me put pen to paper.' (*Letters to William Blackwood and David S. Meldrum*, edited William Blackburn (North Carolina: Duke University Press, 1958), pp. 26–7; letter dated 1 August 1898.) The author's note to the published version discusses the earlier abandonment of the work: 'The contents and the course of the story I had clearly in my mind. But as to the way of presenting the facts, and perhaps in a certain measure as to the nature of the facts themselves, I had many doubts. I mean the telling, representative facts, helpful to carry an idea' (p. viii).

7. For example those relating to the oscillations and tensions in the relationship between Mrs Travers and Lingard.

8. The original title was *The Rescuer: A Tale of Narrow Waters*; this was changed during the early years of its writing to *The Rescue: A Romance of Narrow Waters*. What these permutations and the final title have in common is the enactment of cataclysmic events within a confined and isolated space. For discussion on the evolution of the title, see J. D. Gordan, *Joseph Conrad: The Making of a Novelist* (London: Russell and Russell, 1963; first published 1940).

9. For discussion of Conrad's interest in the history of Brooke of Sarawak, see J. D. Gordan, ibid., Hay and Fleishman, op. cit. and C. T. Watts, editor, *Joseph Conrad's Letters to R. B. Cunninghame Graham* (Cambridge University Press, 1969). In the Appendix to this collection, 'Conrad and the Dowager Ranee

of Sarawak', the wife of a descendant of the original Rajah, Watts suggests that Conrad's reading of the Ranee's *My Life in Sarawak* may conceivably have encouraged him to resume work on and complete *The Rescue*. The fulsome tones of Conrad's letter to the Ranee acknowledging a communication from her in praise of *The Rescue* are a telling contrast to the fictional enterprise which invalidates a legend to which Conrad was personally attracted:

> I am immensely gratified and touched you have been good enough to write to me. The first Rajah has been one of my boyish admirations, a feeling I have kept to this day strengthened by the better understanding of the greatness of his character and the unstained rectitude of his purpose. The book which has found favour in your eyes has been inspired in a great measure by the history of the first Rajah's enterprise and even by the lecture of his journals as partly reproduced by Captain Mundy and others. (Letter dated 15 July 1920; quoted Watts, p. 210.)

10. The Lingard of 'The Rescuer' is cast in more heroic mould than in the final version; the dimensions of his unaided achievement and his chivalry to the Malayan people are emphasised, as are his craving for mastery and danger, his violent propensities and his ambition to make history. All the same, if the Lingard of *The Rescue* is less exorbitant than in the manuscript version, he hardly qualifies as the emasculated character described by Moser, op. cit.

11. Fleishman, op. cit., Chapter IV, 'Colonists and Conquerors', constructs a theory about Conrad's vision of the colonialist committed to the role, place and people amongst whom he lived, as a posture distinguishing him from the conqueror. In the face of the counter-examples advanced by the fiction on the nature of the 'colonist', this argument does not hold up.

12. The Lingard of *An Outcast of the Islands* has precious pictures of his youthful days and the stable heritage within which his benevolent instincts had been nurtured. Despite his ignominious end in *Almayer's Folly*, a victim of his obsessive quest for the fabled gold and diamonds of the islands, Lingard in his prime is recalled as a confident man of action, a stranger to hesitation and failure, single-minded, determined, in possession of moral certainties, a simple, foolish and obtuse person, able to boast that he had never regretted a single action in his life and had been blessed by a wondrous fate. None of this makes sense in *The Rescue*, which is about a man whose deeds and omissions as a young man leave him 'a prey forever to infinite remorse and endless regrets', so that it is inconceivable that he will evolve into the person of the earlier novels.

13. In a letter to Edward Garnett lamenting yet again the difficulties he was having with the original draft, Conrad wrote: 'You see I must justify – give a motive – to my yacht people, the artificial, civilised creatures that are brought in contact with the primitive Lingard'. (*Letters From Conrad: 1895–1924*, edited Edward Garnett (London: The Nonesuch Press, 1928); letter dated 5 August 1896, pp. 42–3.)

14. In 'The Rescuer' these phrases appear respectively as 'white chiefs' and 'all whites', pp. 390, 488. The manuscript version is more explicit on the process of Lingard's betrayal of his dependants, for example see pp. 445, 462.

15. 'The Rescuer' is more explicit about Lingard's shocked discovery that he no longer cares for Immada and Hassim.
16. The 1916 manuscript section has Mrs Travers calculating the necessity of battling for Lingard's devotion against the hold which Hassim and Immada have on him.
17. 'The Rescuer' has Lingard turning on Immada with animosity for addressing Mrs Travers in this manner. Because Mrs Travers's tenderness and compassion for Immada are more apparent in the manuscript version, the meetings between the two women have a different resonance; see pp. 268–9, 439–40.
18. Cf. Fleishman, who maintains that Conrad approved of 'colonists' like Lingard who committed themselves to the place and the people and established relationships of mutual trust and shared interests.
19. In the interests of pursuing the central discussion, it is this aspect that is foregrounded, although it is made clear that the Wajo people, to whom Hassim, Immada and their followers belong, are energetic cultivators, jealous of their independence and with a tradition of struggle against the Dutch.
20. Moser, op. cit., faults *The Rescue* for eliminating the visual imagery of the original and failing to create a symbolic landscape. The opening passage of 'the Rescuer' reads in part:

> There is no peace like the peace of the narrow seas. The great ocean knows not the perfect rest, the unruffled glitter, the smooth repose of seas held in close bondage by the unyielding grasp of enclosing lands . . . And when the night descends upon the narrow waters, – the soft night, the night impalpable and impenetrable, the night – secret and tepid – they lay [sic] under it silent . . . till perchance, the rising moon sends a metallic dart of glittering light to piece with its cold shaft the black heart, the heart pitiless and serene of the tropical night. In their repose the narrow waters are cruel and mute, treacherous and smiling with a perpetual smile of sunny content, a content that knows nothing of the unceasing torment, the immense and bitter unrest which wrings its never-ending moan from the sorrowful depths of great oceans . . . The shallow heart of narrow seas has no mystery for the eyes of the dwellers of the islands; for those dreamy and reckless vagabonds who are its masters. To them it is like a slave; obedient yet rebellious, submissive yet false; an accomplice and an enemy. Such are the narrow seas of the east! Serene, beautiful and false. The great ocean is appalling and irresistible as fate. The narrow seas are cruel and merciless – merciless as spite. (pp. 1–3)

Such writing reads like a parody of early Conrad, and the loss of epithet-laden passages choked with phrases like scented and mysterious islands, cruel, mute, treacherous and smiling seas, the smiling corruption of narrow waters, the foul ground and tropical foliage of the coast, pitiless tropical nights, etc., is a distinct gain to the final version. See for example 'The Rescuer' pp. 5–6, 99–100, 100–1, 242–3, 291, 411–12, 419–20.

21. In 'The Rescuer' this passage has 'is remarkable for the total absence of features' instead of 'has no distinctive features', and 'by the weight of the

overarching sky whose immense dome rests upon it' instead of the wording quoted above.

22. Forster appears to have written only one essay on Conrad, 'Joseph Conrad: A Note' (1920), being a review of *Notes on Life and Letters* reprinted in *Abinger Harvest* (London: Edward Arnold, 1936). *The Rescue* was first published in 1920, a few years before *A Passage to India* and it is possible that Forster had read it; however, fragments of Chapter 12, the first chapter of 'Caves', written in the 1913–14 period, survive, and from these it is clear that the conception developed in the finished work had already been formulated. Oliver Stallybrass considers that a version of the chapter was completed in the earlier period although the published form was written after Forster resumed work on the novel in 1922. See *The Manuscripts of* 'A Passage to India' (London: Edward Arnold, 1978).

23. Part II of 'The Rescuer' is entitled 'Belarab', suggesting that Conrad envisaged a larger role for this character than was to be the case in *The Rescue*. Passages in the manuscript version devoted to his puritanical, fiery religious beliefs and aspirations, do not survive in the final form.

24. In 'A Familiar Preface', *A Personal Record: Some Reminiscences* (1912) Conrad wrote this account of his conception of the artist's vocation:

> I, too, would like to hold the magic wand giving that command over laughter and tears which is declared to be the highest achievement of imaginative literature. Only, to be a great magician, one must surrender oneself to occult and irresponsible powers, either outside or within one's breast. We have all heard of simple men selling their souls for love or power to some grotesque devil. The most ordinary intelligence can perceive without much reflection that anything of that sort is bound to be a fool's bargain. I don't lay claim to particular wisdom because of my dislike and distrust of such transactions. It may be my sea training upon a natural disposition to keep good hold on the one thing really mine, but the fact is that I have a positive horror of losing even for one moment that full possession of myself which is the first condition of good service. And I have carried my notion of good service from my earlier into my later existence. I, who have never sought in the written word anything else but a form of the Beautiful – I have carried over that article of creed from the decks of ships to the more circumscribed space of my desk, and by that act, I suppose, I have become permanently imperfect in the eyes of the ineffable company of pure esthetes. (pp. xviii–xix)

25. Moser's contention, op. cit., that *The Rescue* sanctions Lingard's passive acceptance of repose as the greatest good, would seem to be mistaken.

26. Quoted in Elsa Nettels, *James and Conrad* (Athens, GA: University of Georgia Press, 1977); the letter dated 15 February 1919 is in the Berg Collection.

27. Undated letter, estimated by the editor as having been written at the end of 1918, quoted in Gérard Jean-Aubry, *Joseph Conrad: Life and Letters*, Vol. II, p. 212. The editor adds in a footnote that *The Rescue* was serialised in the American magazine *Romance* between November 1919 and May 1920, and not in *Cosmopolitan*.

CHAPTER 4: *The Nigger of the 'Narcissus'*

1. For an example of this practice, see Vernon Young, 'Trial by Water: Joseph Conrad's *The Nigger of the 'Narcissus'*, in *The Art of Joseph Conrad: A Critical Symposium*, edited R. W. Stallman (1960), first printed in *Accent* (Spring 1952).

2. Jacques Berthoud, *Joseph Conrad: The Major Phase* (Cambridge University Press, 1978), p. 39.

3. Conrad was years later to write again of 'the old tradition of the sea', belief in which was integral to his personal theology:

> Noticed or unnoticed, ignored or commended, they have answered invariably the call to do their work, the very conditions of which made them what they are. They have always served the nation's needs through their own invariable fidelity to the demands of their special life . . . Their work has made them, as work undertaken with single-minded devotion makes men, giving to their achievements that vitality and continuity in which their souls are expressed, tempered and matured through the succeeding generations. ('Tradition' (1918) in *Notes on Life and Letters*, pp. 196–7)

> What spirit was it that inspired the unfailing manifestations of their simple fidelity? . . . Who can tell how a tradition comes into the world? . . . But once it has been born it becomes a spirit. Nothing can extinguish its force then. Clouds of greedy selfishness, the subtle dialectics of revolt and fear, may obscure it for a time, but in very truth it remains an immortal ruler invested with the power of honour and shame. ('Well Done' (1918), ibid., p. 183)

> What in the essays sounds like the sermons of an established author fulfilling an expected function as a pillar of society in a period of national crisis reads quite differently in the fictions, where the articulation of the doctrine resonates with the unction of dogma and the doctrine itself is denied the status of an absolute truth.

4. In 'Expressionism and Working-Class Fiction', *New Left Review*, No. 130 (November–December 1981), Ken Worpole discusses the work of George Garrett who, like Conrad, went to sea and wrote of life at sea, painting, in Worpole's words: 'a picture of utter human desolation and extremity' (p. 90). He also refers to an essay Garrett wrote in *The Adelphi*, in June 1936, on *The Nigger of the 'Narcissus'*, where he takes Conrad to task for loading the dice against Donkin:

> At a number of key points in the story Garrett challenges Conrad's plausibility in the actual details of seafaring practice. Whereas Conrad invites the reader to identify with the Captain and the pride of the shipowners at the expense of the poorly fed, over-worked and miserably paid seaman, Garrett in his critical essay suggests that the reader attempt for a change to identify with the sailors who actually do the work that creates the circumstances for Conrad to write his moral tale . . . At the end

of his essay Garrett looks forward to the day when, 'the Donkins might write the story of the sea. Let's hope it will be to better a world in which shipowners can still send out heavily insured coffin ships and their helpless crews'. (p. 91)

5. Cf. Conrad's recollections of the sea as a cruel adversary recorded in 'The Mirror of the Sea' (1906):

> The sea . . . has no generosity. No display of manly qualities – courage, hardihood, endurance, faithfulness – has ever been known to touch its irresponsible consciousness of power. The ocean has the conscienceless temper of a savage autocrat spoiled by much adulation. He cannot brook the slightest appearance of defiance, and has remained the irreconcilable enemy of ships and men ever since ships and men had the un-heard of audacity to go afloat together in the face of his frown . . . The most amazing wonder of the deep is its unfathomable cruelty. (p. 137)

6. Ian Watt, *Conrad in the Nineteenth Century* (Chatto and Windus, 1980), p. 125. For Watt 'the heroic figure of Singleton' is associated with 'the millennial continuity of human solidarity . . . Unlike other members of the crew of the *Narcissus*, Singleton is absolute in his unthinking commitment to the spirit of a simpler phase of society' (p. 123). Cf. Tony Tanner, 'Butterflies and Beetles – Conrad's Two Truths' in *Twentieth Century Interpretations of Lord Jim: A Collection of Critical Essays*, edited Robert E. Kuehn (New Jersey: Prentice-Hall, 1969), first published *Chicago Review*, xvi, No. 1 (1963), who writes of Conrad's presentation of Singleton: 'It makes it seem as though he were acting in unflinching compliance with a categorical imperative. The particularly Conradian aspect of this concept of duty is the fact that he can no longer produce the sanctions and proofs which would justify and endorse the standards of conduct which he nevertheless feels to be "imperative" ' (p. 66–7).

7. A term that originated as a description by a master race of peoples who were socially subordinate and regarded as racially inferior, was never anything but racist, and to argue that the word has accreted offensive connotations only in recent times is disingenuous.

8. The function of Wait's blackness in the fiction has been given various interpretations: Michael J. C. Echeruo, *The Conditioned Imagination From Shakespeare to Conrad: Studies in the Exo-Cultural Stereotype* (London: Macmillan, 1978), who argues that the seriousness of a work of literature is directly the function of the force of the conditioning frenzy or prejudice, maintains that Wait is symbolic not in the ordinary sense of representing an abstract idea, but in the special sense that 'Conrad asserts a correspondence . . . between the imaginative predispositions of his European audience to this black sailor and his realised role in the novel'. Since Conrad is dependent for the presentation of Wait on the long-standing association of the black person with the brute and of physical blackness with moral darkness, 'the symbolic power of Wait's blackness is not a metaphoric construct but a kind of brutal fact to which Conrad draws attention in the story' (quotations from pp. 101, 103). Vernon Young in 'Trial by Water', op. cit., accounts for Conrad's racism by claiming that his experience with African 'savages' justified his

using the type as illustrative of the black-magical and the 'unevolved'. When describing Wait's face, Young continues, Conrad 'was enjoying the privilege, apparently inevitable to their psychology, which the white races have taken upon themselves, of seeing the dark races as either exotic or sinister but in any case inferior' (p. 114).

9. Watt, op. cit., who finds that Conrad's picture of the crew has affinities with the thought of Tönnies (1865–1936) and Durkheim (1858–1917), reads the tensions on board ship as embodying the division between the old *Gemeinschaft* governed by customary procedure and traditional hierarchies, and the new order of the *Gesellschaft* society which arises from the free, conscious, rational and willed choice of its members.

CHAPTER 5: *Lord Jim*

1. Cf. Dorothy Van Ghent, who sees in the fissured hills an image of Jim's condition: 'He is not only an outcast from his own kind but he is also an outcast from himself, cloven spiritually, unable to recognise his own identity, separated from himself as the two halves of the hills are separated'. 'On *Lord Jim*' in *Twentieth Century Interpretations of Lord Jim, A Collection of Critical Essays*, edited Robert E. Kuehn (New Jersey: Prentice-Hall, 1969), p. 75; essay first published in *The English Novel: Form and Function* (New York: Holt, Rhinehart and Winston, 1953).

2. See Stephen Zelnick, 'Conrad's *Lord Jim*: Meditations On The Other Hemisphere', *The Minnesota Review*, No. 11 (Fall 1978). Even if Zelnick does interpret the novel too exclusively as a critique of imperialism, his essay remains essential reading on a work that has too often been emptied of its historical meanings in critical discussion.

3. This is an obvious example of how Conrad's fictions interrogate bald declarations made in his prose writing – cf. 'Those who read me know my conviction that the world, the temporal world, rests on a few very simple ideas; so simple that they must be as old as the hills. It rests notably, among others, on the idea of Fidelity'. 'A Familiar Preface' to *A Personal Record*, p. xxi.

4. Irving Howe writes: 'In the contrast between what Marlow says and what he tells, lies the distance Conrad can allow between the stoical norm and the romantic deviation; which is to say, between the desire to cling to moral formulae and the recognition that modern life cannot be lived by them, between the demands of social conscience and the freed fantasies of the idyllic or the dangerous, between the commandments of one's fathers and the quandries of exile'. 'Conrad: Order and Anarchy', *Politics and the Novel* (New York: Horizon Press, 1957), pp. 81–2; essay first published in *Kenyon Review* (Autumn 1953) and (Winter 1954).

5. For Albert Guerard, in *Conrad the Novelist* (Oxford University Press, 1958), the fog, mist and moonlight in which Jim is seen signifies Jim's self-deception and not Marlow's perception.

6. The tendency in critical discussion to see in the French Lieutenant one of Conrad's intended exemplary figures is hard to maintain in the light of the equivocal representation.

7. Jeremy Hawthorn, op. cit., argues that one meaning of 'one of us' is the solidarity of colonialists in their relationship to the colonised.
8. Ian Watt, *Conrad in the Nineteenth Century* (Chatto and Windus, 1980).

CHAPTER 6: *Nostromo*

1. *Beginnings: Intention and Method* (New York: Basic Books, 1975) p. 110.
2. The sources on which Conrad drew in his construction of Costaguana and its history are discussed *inter alia* by Fleishman, who cites the writings of George Frederick Masterman, E. B. Eastwick and Ramon Paez. A major source and influence was the work of Cunninghame Graham; see *Cunninghame Graham: A Critical Biography*, C. T. Watts and Laurence Davies (Cambridge University Press, 1979).
3. See Roger L. Cox, 'Conrad's Nostromo as Boatswain', *Modern Language Notes*, 74 (April 1954).
4. See Peter Christmas, 'Conrad's *Nostromo*: A Tale of Europe', *Literature and History*, 6, No. 1 (Spring 1980) who considers that the concept of ownership lies at the heart of the title and constitutes its principal meaning.
5.   Surely there is a mine for silver, and a place for gold which they refine . . .
    But where shall wisdom be found? and where is the place of understanding? Man knoweth not the price thereof; neither is it found in the land of the living . . .
    It cannot be gotten for gold, neither shall silver be weighed for the price thereof . . .
    When then cometh wisdom? and where is the place of understanding? . . .
    God understandeth the way thereof, and he knoweth the place thereof.
    (Job 28: 1, 12, 13, 15, 20, 23)
6. *Notes on Life and Letters.*
7. This reproduces the received view of the American Indians as inert, apathetic, docile and passive. In *The Lords of Human Kind: European attitudes to the outside world in the imperial age* (Harmondsworth: Penguin, 1972, first published London: Weidenfeld and Nicholson, 1969), V. G. Kiernan writes: 'To the white man there was a more than Oriental impenetrability in these subject races, and a fatalistic apathy that must have been induced in them by ordeals of recent centuries was frequently regarded as an innate Amerindian quality' (p. 290). Kiernan shows how western observers in the nineteenth century saw this ruling trait of the Amerindians as an apathy and inertia which must inevitably lead to the extinction of the race.
8. In his discussion of South America through European eyes, Kiernan, ibid., cites evidence of Latin Americans seen as pretentious, undisciplined, shiftless, fierce, cowardly and decadent.
9. See E. J. Hobsbawn, *The Age of Revolution 1789–1848* (London: Weidenfeld and Nicholson, 1962) on European interests in Latin America.
10. *The Protestant Ethic and the Spirit of Capitalism* (London: Unwin, 1930) translated by Talcott Parsons with an Introduction by R. W. Tawney. The essays were first published in 1904 and 1905. See also R. W. Tawney, *Religion and the Rise of Capitalism* (London: John Murray, 1926).
11. The phrase was apparently coined by R. Cunninghame Graham, who wrote

books on Latin American politics at the turn of the century in which he compared the interventions of the United States to those of the early *conquistadores* and emphasised the hypocrisy and futility of attempting to found a durable and decent moral order on the basis of 'material interests'. See Watts and Davies, op. cit.

CONCLUSION

1. J. A. Hobson, *Imperialism* (London: Allen and Unwin, 1938, first published 1902).
2. See V. G. Kiernan, ibid., who quotes the protest of Belfort Bax against his fellow-socialists, p. 8. See also previous references to the dissent of R. Cunninghame Graham.
3. See for example, G. P. Gooch, 'Imperialism' in *The Heart of the Empire*; edited C. F. G. Masterman (London: T. Fisher Unwin, 1901, reprinted Sussex: The Harvester Press, 1973); J. M. Robertson, *Patriotism and Empire* (London: Grant Richards, 1899), and J. A. Hobson, op. cit.

Bibliography

Conrad's Writings
References are to the Medallion Edition 1925–28 which has the same pagination as the Uniform and Collected Editions of *The Works of Joseph Conrad* (Dent).

Almayer's Folly (1895)
An Outcast of the Islands (1896)
The Nigger of the 'Narcissus' (1897)
Heart of Darkness (1899) in *Youth: A Narrative and Two Other Stories* (1902)
Lord Jim (1900)
The Inheritors (1901)
Nostromo (1904)
The Rescue (1920)
The Mirror of the Sea (1906)
A Personal Record (1912)
Notes on Life and Letters (1921)
'The Rescuer' Manuscript, *Ashley Library 4787*, British Museum

Selected Works on and Relating to Conrad's Fiction

Jocelyn Baines, *Joseph Conrad: A Critical Biography* (London: Weidenfeld and Nicholson, 1960)
Jacques Berthoud, *Joseph Conrad: The Major Phase* (Cambridge: Cambridge University Press, 1978)
William Blackburn, editor, *Joseph Conrad: Letters to William Blackwood and David S. Meldrum* (North Carolina: Duke University Press, 1958)
Peter Christmas, 'Conrad's *Nostromo*: A Tale of Europe', *Literature and History*, 6, No. 1 (Spring 1980)
C. B. Cox, *Joseph Conrad: The Modern Imagination* (London: Dent, 1974)

Roger L. Cox, 'Conrad's Nostromo as Boatswain', *Modern Language Notes*, 74 (April 1970)

H. M. Daleski, *Joseph Conrad: The Way of Dispossession* (London: Faber, 1977)

Jacques Darras, *Joseph Conrad and the West: Signs of Empire* (London: Macmillan, 1981)

Leonard F. Dean, editor, *Joseph Conrad's Heart of Darkness: Backgrounds and Criticism* (New Jersey: Prentice-Hall, 1960)

M. J. C. Echeruo, *The Conditioned Imagination from Shakespeare to Conrad: Studies in the Exo-cultural Stereotype* (London: Macmillan, 1978)

Avrom Fleishman, *Conrad's Politics: Community and Anarchy in the Fiction of Joseph Conrad* (Baltimore: Johns Hopkins, 1967)

Edward Garnett, editor, *Letters from Conrad 1895–1924* (London: The Nonesuch Press, 1928)

R. A. Gekoski, *Conrad, The Moral World of the Novelist* (London: Paul Elek, 1978)

J. D. Gordan, *Joseph Conrad: The Making of a Novelist* (London: Russell and Russell, 1963, first published 1940)

Albert J. Guerard, *Conrad the Novelist* (Oxford: Oxford University Press, 1958)

Robert D. Hamner, *Joseph Conrad and the Colonial World. A Selected Bibliography*. Conradiana, xiv, No. 3 (1982)

Hunt Hawkins, 'Conrad's Critique of Imperialism in *Heart of Darkness*', *PMLA* 94, No. 2 (1979)

Jeremy Hawthorn, *Joseph Conrad: Language and Fictional Self-consciousness* (London: Edward Arnold, 1979)

Eloise Knapp Hay, *The Political Novels of Joseph Conrad: A Critical Study* (Chicago: University of Chicago Press, 1963)

Douglas Hewitt, *Conrad: A Reassessment* (London: Bowes and Bowes, 1968, first published 1952)

Irving Howe, *Politics and the Novel* (New York: Horizon Press, 1957)

Gérard Jean-Aubry, *Joseph Conrad in the Congo* (New York: Haskell House, 1973, first published 1926)

——, Joseph Conrad: *Life and Letters* (London: Heinemann, 1927)

——, *The Sea Dreamer: A Definitive Biography of Joseph Conrad* (London: Allen and Unwin, 1957)

Gareth Jenkins, 'Conrad's *Nostromo* and History', *Literature and History*, No. 6 (Autumn 1977)

Bruce Johnson, *Conrad's Models of Mind* (Minneapolis: University of Minnesota Press, 1971)

Frederick Karl, *Joseph Conrad: The Three Lives* (London: Faber, 1979)

——, 'Conrad Studies', review essay in *Studies in the Novel*, 9, No. 3 (Fall 1977)

R. Kimbrough, editor, *Heart of Darkness: An Authoritative Text, Backgrounds and Sources, Essays in Criticism* (New York, Norton, 1963)

Robert E. Kuehn, editor, *Twentieth Century Interpretations of Lord Jim, A Collection of Critical Essays* (New Jersey: Prentice-Hall, 1969)

John A. McClure, 'The Rhetoric of Restraint: *Heart of Darkness*', *Nineteenth Century Fiction*, 32, No. 3 (1977)

J. Hillis Miller, *Poets of Reality* (Oxford: Oxford University Press, 1966)

Thomas Moser, *Joseph Conrad: Achievement and Decline* (Oxford: Oxford University Press, 1957)

——, ' "The Rescuer" Manuscript: A Key to Conrad's Development – and Decline', *Harvard Library Bulletin* (Autumn 1956)

V. S. Naipaul, *The Return of Eva Peron* (London: Deutsch, 1980)

Zdzislaw Najder, editor, *Conrad's Polish Background* (Oxford: Oxford University Press, 1964)

Elsa Nettels, *James and Conrad* (Athens, GA: University of Georgia Press, 1977)

Jonah Raskin, 'Imperialism: Conrad's *Heart of Darkness*', *Journal of Contemporary History*, 2, No. 2 (1967)

Claire Rosenfield, *Paradise of Snakes: An Archetypal Analysis of Conrad's Political Novels* (Chicago: University of Chicago Press, 1967)

Royal Roussel, *The Metaphysics of Darkness: A Study in the Development of Conrad's Fiction* (Baltimore: Johns Hopkins, 1971)

K. K. Ruthven, 'The Savage God: Conrad and Lawrence', *Critical Quarterly*, x, Nos 1 and 2 (1968)

Edward W. Said, *Joseph Conrad and the Fiction of Autobiography* (Cambridge, Mass: Harvard, 1966)

Norman Sherry, *Conrad's Eastern World* (Cambridge: Cambridge University Press, 1966)

——, editor, *Conrad: The Critical Heritage* (London: Routledge and Kegan Paul, 1973)

——, editor, *Joseph Conrad: A Commemoration* (Papers for the 1974

International Conference on Conrad) (London: Macmillan, 1976)

R. W. Stallman, editor, *The Art of Joseph Conrad: A Critical Symposium* (East Lansing: Michigan State University Press, 1960)

Tony Tanner, *Conrad's Lord Jim* (London: Arnold, 1963)

——, ' "Gnawed Bones" and "Artless Tales": Eating and Narrative in Conrad', in *Joseph Conrad: A Commemoration*, edited Sherry (1966)

——, 'Butterflies and Beetles – Conrad's Two Truths' in *Twentieth Century Interpretations of Lord Jim, A Collection of Critical Essays*, edited Kuehn (1969)

Bruce E. Teets and Helmut E. Gerber, *Joseph Conrad: An Annotated Bibliography of Writings About Him* (De Kalb: North Illinois University Press, 1971)

Dorothy Van Ghent, 'On *Lord Jim*' in *Twentieth Century Interpretations of Lord Jim, A Collection of Critical Essays*, edited Kuehn (1969)

Ian Watt, *Conrad in the Nineteenth Century* (Chatto and Windus, 1980)

——, '*Heart of Darkness* and Nineteenth Century Thought', *Partisan Review*, XLV (1978)

C. T. Watts, editor, *Joseph Conrad's Letters to R. B. Cunninghame Graham* (Cambridge: Cambridge University Press, 1969)

——, *Conrad's Heart of Darkness: A Critical and Contextual Discussion* (Milan: Mursia International, 1977)

C. T. Watts and Laurence Davies, *Cunninghame Graham: A Critical Biography* (Cambridge: Cambridge University Press, 1979)

Raymond Williams, *The English Novel from Dickens to Lawrence* (London: Chatto and Windus, 1971)

Vernon Young, 'Lingard's Folly: The Lost Subject', *Kenyon Review*, 15 (1953)

——, 'Trial by Water: Joseph Conrad's *The Nigger of the 'Narcissus'*, in *The Art of Joseph Conrad*, edited Stallman (1960)

Stephen Zelnick, 'Conrad's *Lord Jim*: Meditations on the Other Hemisphere', *The Minnesota Review*, No. 11 (Fall 1978)

Studies on Literature and Imperialism

Martin Green, *Dreams of Adventure, Deeds of Empire* (London: Routledge and Kegan Paul, 1980)

Allen J. Greenberger, *The British Image of India: A Study in the Literature of Imperialism* (London: Oxford University Press, 1969)

D. C. R. À. Goonetilleke, *Developing Countries in British Fiction* (London: Macmillan, 1977)

Susanne Howe, *Novels of Empire* (New York: Columbia University Press, 1949)

M. M. Mahood, *The Colonial Encounter: A reading of six novels* (London: Rex Collings, 1977)

John A. McClure, *Kipling and Conrad: The Colonial Fiction* (Cambridge, Mass. and London: Harvard University Press, 1981)

Jeffrey Meyers, *Fiction and the Colonial Experience* (Ipswich: The Boydell Press, 1973)

Benita Parry, *Delusions and Discoveries: Studies on India in the British Imagination 1880–1930* (London: Allen Lane, The Penguin Press, 1972)

Jonah Raskin, *The Mythology of Imperialism* (New York: Random House, 1971)

Jeffrey Richards, 'The Cinema of Empire' in *Visions of Yesterday* (London: Routledge and Kegan Paul, 1973)

Alan Sandison, *The Wheel of Empire: A Study of the Imperial Idea in Some Late Nineteenth and Early Twentieth Century Fiction* (London: Macmillan, 1967)

Brian V. Street, *The Savage in Literature: Representations of 'primitive' society in English fiction 1858–1920* (London: Routledge and Kegan Paul, 1975)

Works on Theories of Imperialism

G. P. Gooch, 'Imperialism' in *The Heart of Empire*, edited C. F. G. Masterman (London: T. Fisher Unwin, 1901; reprinted Sussex: The Harvester Press, 1973)

J. A. Hobson, *Imperialism: A Study* (London: Allen and Unwin, 1938, first published 1902)

T. Kemp, *Theories of Imperialism* (London: Dobson Books, 1967)

V. G. Kiernan, *Marxism and Imperialism* (London: Arnold, 1974)

R. Koebner and H. Schmidt, *Imperialism: the story and significance of a political word 1840–1960* (Cambridge: Cambridge University Press, 1964)

V. I. Lenin, *Imperialism, the Highest Stage of Capitalism, A Popular*

Outline (London: Lawrence and Wishart, 1933, first published 1917)

George Lichtheim, *Imperialism* (London: Allen Lane, the Penguin Press, 1971)

Roger Owen and Bob Sutcliffe, editors, *Studies in the Theory of Imperialism* (London: Longman, 1972)

J. M. Robertson, *Patriotism and Empire* (London: Grant Richards, 1899)

A. P. Thornton, *Doctrines of Imperialism* (New York: John Wiley, 1965)

Robin Winks, editor, *The Age of Imperialism* (New Jersey: Prentice-Hall, 1969)

Western Perception of the Other Hemisphere and The Reactions of the Non-western worlds

Chinua Achebe: *Morning Yet on Creation Day* (London: Heinemann, 1975)

Henri Baudet, *Paradise on Earth: Some Thoughts on European Images of Non-European Man* (New Haven, Conn. and London: Yale University Press, 1965)

Marion Berghahn, *Images of Africa in Black American Literature* (London: Macmillan, 1977)

Christine Bolt, *Victorian Attitudes to Race* (London: Routledge and Kegan Paul, 1971)

Philip Curtin, *The Image of Africa* (London: Macmillan, 1965)

Frantz Fanon, *The Wretched of The Earth* (London: MacGibbon and Kee, 1965, first published in France 1961)

——, *A Dying Colonialism* (New York: Grove Press, 1967 first published in France 1959)

——, *Black Skin, White Masks* (New York: Grove Press, 1967, first published in France 1952)

——, *Toward the African Revolution* (New York: Grove Press, 1967, first published in France 1964)

Marvin Harris, *The Rise of Anthropological Theory* (London: Routledge and Kegan Paul, 1969)

V. G. Kiernan, *The Lords of Human Kind: European attitudes to the outside world in the imperial age* (Harmondsworth: Penguin Books, 1972, first published London: Weidenfeld and Nicholson, 1969)

O. Mannoni, *Prospero and Caliban: The Psychology of Colonization* (New York: Praeger, 1956, first published in France 1950)

Albert Memmi, *The Colonizer and the Colonized* (Boston: Beacon Press, 1965, first published in France 1957)

——, *Dominated Man* (Boston: Beacon Press, 1968)

Edward W. Said, *Orientalism* (London: Routledge and Kegan Paul, 1978)

General Bibliography

Louis Althusser, *Lenin and Philosophy and Other Essays*, translated Ben Brewster (London: New Left Books, 1971)

Tony Bennett, *Formalism and Marxism* (London: Methuen, 1979)

Hugh Cunningham, 'The Language of Patriotism, 1750–1914', *History Workshop*, Issue 12 (Autumn 1981)

Terry Eagleton, *Marxism and Literary Criticism* (London: Methuen, 1976)

——, *Criticism and Ideology: A Study in Marxist Literary Theory* (London: New Left Books, 1976)

——, *Walter Benjamin or Towards a Revolutionary Criticism* (London: New Left Books, 1981)

Wayne Hudson, *The Marxist Philosophy of Ernst Bloch* (London: Macmillan 1982)

Fredric Jameson, *Marxism and Form: Twentieth Century Dialectical Theories of Literature* (Princeton, New Jersey: Princeton University Press, 1971)

——, *The Political Unconscious: Narrative as a Socially Symbolic Act* (London: Methuen, 1981)

Herbert Marcuse, *Eros and Civilisation: A Philosophical Inquiry Into Freud* (Boston, Mass.: Beacon Press, 1955)

S. S. Prawer, *Marxism and World Literature* (Oxford: Oxford University Press, 1978)

Edward Said, *Beginnings: Intention and Method* (New York: Basic Books, 1975)

Cliff Slaughter, *Marxism, Ideology and Literature* (London: Macmillan, 1980)

R. W. Tawney, *Religion and the Rise of Capitalism* (London: John Murray, 1926)

Ken Warpole, 'Expressionism and Working Class Fiction', *New Left Review*, No. 130 (November–December, 1981)

Max Weber, *The Protestant Ethic and the Spirit of Capitalism*, translated Talcott Parsons (London: Unwin, 1930, essays first published in journals in 1904 and 1905)

Raymond Williams, *Marxism and Literature* (Oxford: Oxford University Press, 1977)

——, *Problems in Materialism and Culture* (London: Verso Editions and New Left Books, 1980)

Index